The Abingdon Religious Education Texts
David G. Downey, General Editor

COLLEGE SERIES GEORGE HERBERT BETTS, Editor

The Ethical Teaching of the Gospels

By
ERNEST WARD BURCH
Assistant Professor of New Testament Interpretation in Garrett Biblical Institute

THE ABINGDON PRESS
NEW YORK CINCINNATI

Printed in the United States of America

TO MY WIFE
HARRIET SQUIRE BURCH

CONTENTS

CHAPTER I

THE HISTORICAL APPROACH TO THE ETHICAL TEACHING OF JESUS

CHAPTER II

THE ETHICS OF THE GOSPEL ACCORDING TO MARK

CHAPTER III

THE ETHICS OF THE GOSPEL ACCORDING TO MATTHEW

CHAPTER IV

THE ETHICS OF THE GOSPEL ACCORDING TO LUKE

CHAPTER V

THE ETHICS OF THE GOSPEL ACCORDING TO JOHN

CHAPTER VI

THE ETHICS OF THE GOSPELS AND THE ETHICS OF JESUS

A SELECTED LIST OF BOOKS SUGGESTED FOR COLLATERAL READING

I. The Sources

Burton and Goodspeed:	*A Harmony of the Synoptic Gospels.*
Ernest DeWitt Burton:	*The Teaching of Jesus: A Source Book.*
Doremus Almy Hayes:	*The Synoptic Gospels and the Book of Acts.*
Maurice Jones:	*The Four Gospels.*
Gustav Dalman:	*The Words of Jesus.*
F. Crawford Burkitt:	*The Gospel History and Its Transmission.*
A. Huck:	*Synopsis of the First Three Gospels.*

II. Background

Hinckley G. Mitchell:	*The Ethics of the Old Testament.*
John M. P. Smith:	*The Moral Life of the Hebrews.*
Thomas Walker:	*The Teaching of Jesus and the Jewish Teaching of His Age.*
Robert Henry Charles:	*Religious Development Between the Old Testament and the New Testament.*
Edward Chisholm Dewick:	*Primitive Christian Eschatology.*

III. The Teaching of Jesus

Heinrich H. Wendt:	*The Teaching of Jesus.*
Alexander B. Bruce:	*The Kingdom of God.*
Edward I. Bosworth:	*The Life and Teaching of Jesus.*
Henry Churchill King:	*The Ethics of Jesus.*
Ernest Findlay Scott:	*The Ethical Teaching of Jesus.*
J. Alexander Findlay:	*The Realism of Jesus.*
Henry Clay Vedder:	*The Fundamentals of Christianity.*
Samuel Dickey:	*The Constructive Revolution of Jesus.*

IV. Present Problems

Walter Rauschenbusch:	*Christianizing the Social Order.*
	The Social Principles of Jesus.
Shailer Mathews:	*The Church and the Changing Order.*
Charles Abram Ellwood:	*The Reconstruction of Religion.*
	Christianity and Social Science.

PREFACE

THIS text book deals with one portion of the contents of the New Testament. Its field is purposely restricted to the ethical teaching found in the Four Gospels, that is, the moral instruction or appeal ascribed by the gospel writers to Jesus of Nazareth.

Included under the term "ethical teaching" are all those precepts which have as their aim the ennobling of human experience and the development of personal character. Likewise all that is clearly designed to teach men how to live together and how best to develop those bonds of social amity which furnish high satisfaction in the community life is ethical in character. The term properly includes all that is proposed for the establishment and regulation of family life, all that embraces the manifold social relations of the individual and of various groups, large and small, whether within racial and national boundaries or outside such limits. All that involves human behavior in its motives, its influence, its social significance, and all that treats of human values, in terms of person and character, is ethical in nature.

The word "moral" is here considered synonymous with "ethical" and the two words are used in the same sense throughout the book.

Some of the teaching ascribed to Jesus is more distinctly religious in character. Some teaching in the Gospels may merit even the term "theological." Such portions as those in which Jesus illustrates the providential care of the Father for his children are so simple yet so sublime as to surpass much teaching clothed in more profound terms. The faith of Jesus is at once the most childlike and the most potent. The person of Jesus stands out clearly from the gospel page as that of One who in a real sense is more than human, for the modern reader of the Gospels experiences the compelling force of ages of worship and adoration of Jesus Christ behind the intrinsic power of his words.

To other volumes, however, must be entrusted the exposition of Jesus' teaching about God and religion as such, and discussion of the person of Christ must await another time. These themes are weighty and pressing, but in this study are necessarily omitted.

Throughout the following pages Jesus is thought of primarily as the Teacher of men, certain Jewish men whom he trained and sent out to carry his ringing message to others. They heralded the approach of a new moral order in which shepherdless sheep would be cared for, in which selfish exploitation of men would give place to unselfish fraternal cooperation, in which men should indeed become sons of the Father.

This restriction of viewpoint and material is made in the interest of clear exposition of the moral thought of Jesus, but the observance of this restriction may not be assumed by the student to reflect any actual limitation of Jesus himself in the mind of the writer.

It is earnestly hoped that the method here used will greatly stimulate first-hand study of the Gospels, for in no other way can the student hope to gain any real mastery of the thought of Jesus and his immediate followers.

PREFACE

Among the research questions scattered through the text there are some which encourage the student to make a modern application of the gospel teaching. The text itself, however, is not committed to any such attempt. Attention is focussed upon the meaning of the evangelist.

Few references to modern works upon the teaching of Jesus will be found in the following pages, while many references to the Gospels are offered. The writer owes a great debt of gratitude to all his predecessors in this field, and gratefully acknowledges that indebtedness. In the preparation of this textbook, however, a serious attempt has been made to deal chiefly with the Gospels in Greek and to avoid the compilation method.

Both translation and paraphrase have been used in giving the content of shorter or longer passages. For these renderings the writer assumes all the responsibility. They are offered not so much as examples of fine literary expression as of plain statement of the meaning which the Greek words probably presented to their first readers.

If the book shall prove useful in its intended field and if it shall in any way make clearer to students of the Gospel the intensely social message of Jesus to his times, to that extent the hopes which go with its publication will be fulfilled.

ERNEST WARD BURCH.

Garrett Biblical Institute, Evanston, Illinois.

CHAPTER I

THE HISTORICAL APPROACH TO THE ETHICAL TEACHING OF JESUS

Jesus a Teacher of Ethics

Jesus of Nazareth was a teacher of ethics. He was reared within the Jewish church, whose teachers very earnestly considered problems of conduct, as their wisdom literature abundantly testifies. In the course of his Bible instruction Jesus doubtless became familiar with the contents of books both within and without the Old Testament, many of which contained fine ethical traditions. By no means the least of these books of morals were those that bore the names of the so-called "ethical prophets," Amos, Hosea, Isaiah and Micah, from the eighth and seventh centuries before his time.

Jesus was more than a teacher of morals. He was a moral leader. Men who committed his teaching to writing and at the same time revealed their impressions of his personality assure their readers that the man was indeed the message. He taught in terms that are clear and crystal-like, he had insight that appealed to his companions as unfailing, and his spirit was charmingly frank and sincere. He did not stand aloof from men and their daily toil but himself met every typical human experience. He challenged the loyalty of those whom he called, he mystified some who stood high in the councils of his people, he sometimes terrified those who loved him best by the majesty of his presence and the power of his word, yet all knew the Teacher as a man among men and as one who somehow possessed the inherent right to lead them. By some he was supposed to be a revolutionist, by others he was known to be a builder of character; by some he was persecuted but by most he was loved. His teaching was new in that it focussed a bright light upon many a forgotten truth; it was old in that it affirmed the age-old truth of the law and the prophets in their noble moral insight. The Master was thus an illustration of his own saying: "Every scribe who has been made a disciple in the kingdom of heaven is like a householder who produces from his treasure store new things and old."[1]

Jesus was not only a moral leader for his times, he was a teacher of all who aspire in any time to become moral teachers or leaders. His teaching, imbedded in the Four Gospels, possesses a high degree of interest for all who feel the need of social redemption now. For the moral thought and teaching of Jesus, more than that of any other, when clearly understood, will make social redemption possible.

The student's approach to Jesus the Teacher is through the pages of the Gospels, no word of which was written by the Master himself. The approved method of study is the historical. To listen to the voice of Jesus through the atmosphere of creed or dogma is to risk much of its clearness of tone. To follow tradition alone is to risk the substitution of theological or ecclesiastical bias for the naive and, on the whole, very plain statements of Jesus' sympathetic friends.

---

[1] Matt. 13. 52.

ETHICAL TEACHING OF JESUS

The Historical Approach

The historical procedure is to go directly to the words of the evangelists Mark, Matthew, Luke, and John, studying each one inductively, estimating each one's understanding of the moral message of Jesus, then putting together the results of that study. This book is entitled *The Ethical Teaching of the Gospels* because the contribution of each and all the Gospels must be made before the ethics of Jesus can be formulated. Each Gospel stands for itself, yet all the Gospels stand together. Each evangelist writes for his own circle of readers, yet historically tested, as all the Gospels have been, they are found to present a coherent and symmetrical account of the man of Nazareth and his message.

The Chief Problems

The chief problems to be encountered will be those of analysis and interpretation. It is not desirable to occupy the student's attention with the details of synoptic criticism, nor even with many points of special introduction. Without asking at present about the literary history of the Gospels, each one of the four is to be considered as a unitary work, presenting in its finished form a certain view of the ethical message imparted to the first disciples and kept alive somehow until the day when the gospel writer sent it from his hand to his first readers.

The several writings involved came from widely separated places, from Rome and from Ephesus, from Syria and from Macedonia. Their times also varied from the seventh to the tenth decade of the first century. One who reads the Gospels induc tively lets the writer say what he will, and does not import into the Oriental, first-century work any Western, modern thought. The student will assume that the developing thought of the early church may be reflected in the several Gospels, which will then offer different points of view and varying degrees of emphasis upon certain teaching. The historical method will allow even for discrepancies, although it never creates discrepancies.

Summarizing what has been said, an inductive study of each of the Gospels will result in a detailed statement of Jesus' ethical teaching as it was understood by these men, who were not all eyewitnesses of his ministry on earth. Each evangelist is most probably to be regarded as setting forth the Christian ethics of his time and of his own church. But in any case the ethical teaching of Jesus is the foundation of such Christian ethics and can, to a high degree of certainty, be derived from the later teaching, that is, the ethical teaching of the Gospel writer himself.

At the close of the study[2] the relation of the evangelists' teaching to that of Jesus will be traced by means of well-established literary historical principles. This synthesis will reveal to what extent the ethics of the Gospels is really the ethical teaching of Jesus.

Assignments for Class Reports

1. What is the nature of the study known as "ethics"?
2. How far into the past can one trace the history of ethical study?

---

[2] Chapter VI, pp. 214ff.

3. What claim has Jesus, as a teacher of ethics, upon the interest of a college student?
4. Discover and report upon the titles and the nature of two or three Jewish writings that deal with moral truth and which probably were available in Jesus' day. Are any such works found outside the Bible?
5. What is New Testament Introduction?
6. Report upon the usually accepted dates for the Four Gospels, noting in case of a difference of opinion the earliest and latest proposed dates for each.
7. Indicate the nature of the inductive method in any study.
8. Present in a few paragraphs your statement of the literary historical method of approach to the study of the Gospels.

CHAPTER II

THE ETHICS OF THE GOSPEL ACCORDING TO MARK

Analysis of the Discourse Element in Mark

It is frequently assumed by writers in the New Testament field that the amount of discourse material in Mark is negligible, apart from the parables of the fourth chapter and the apocalypse of the thirteenth. To be sure, in a number of places,[1] the Second Evangelist tells that Jesus taught, omitting the content of such instruction, but in many other places the teaching is set forth in detail. This section will contain a statistical survey of such teaching in the second Gospel.

In chapters 4, 12 and 13 the longest sections containing words of Jesus are found. Many words of the Master in the Gospel are in the nature of dialog designed chiefly to carry the story, and there are a number of sayings that appear somewhat isolated, But when all these are properly appraised there remains a significant body of teaching placed by the Evangelist upon the lips of Jesus, which properly represents the Evangelist's understanding of Jesus' moral views.

The Second Gospel contains about 11,270 words.[2] Of these, 4,006 are words of Jesus, of which all but

[1] Mark 1. 21f.; 2. 2c, 13b; 4. 33; 6. 2, 6b, 34; 10.1.

[2] The count is upon the basis of the Greek text of Westcott and Hort.

eighty-four are direct discourse. In chapter 13 are found 538 words of Jesus, the balance in direct discourse, 3,384, being outside that apocalypse.

Leaving chapter 13 out of consideration for the moment, these 3,384 words of Jesus are distributed through the other fifteen chapters of Mark in about 112 groups, each group containing from one word[3] to 359.[4]

Such a proportion of words of Jesus introduced into the dramatic narrative of Mark shows that the evangelist had an interest in setting forth the substance of Jesus' thought as well as the manner of his life. It often occurs that after a few words of Jesus which serve simply to carry the story (dialog), the evangelist introduces some important teaching.[5]

The words placed by Mark upon Jesus' lips that serve chiefly to "carry the story," as his part of ordinary dialog, excluding strictly "teaching material," number about 676 for the entire Gospel, 291 of these being in chapter 14, sixteen in chapter 13, the remaining 369 being found in chapters 1–12, inclusive, and 15.

Many of Jesus' words in this Gospel are cast into the form of interrogation. Aside from 13.2, the apocalyptic chapter contains not a question, but within the other chapters there are found sixty-two questions upon the lips of Jesus.[6] This fact may be explained by the tendency of the evangelist thus to express his conception of Jesus' method. It is noticeable that in parallel passages Matthew

---

[3] "Ephphatha," 7. 34.

[4] Explanation of parables, 4. 11–32.

[5] Examples are numerous. See Mark 3. 31–35; 8. 17f.; 9. 21, 23; 10. 3, 5ff.; often in chapter 14.

[6] Punction of Westcott and Hort.

frequently omits the question, often substituting statement of fact.

The use of passages in Mark from the Old Testament in Greek offers opportunity for an inquiry as to the relative proportion of such quotations. Of the 4,006 words of Jesus in the second Gospel, 379 are in the form of quotation from the Old Testament.[7]

The student will have noted by this time that chapter 13 of the second Gospel offers certain peculiarities, differentiating it from the rest of the work. Its teaching is decidedly of a different sort; it makes use of a higher percentage of Old Testament material; only one question is found on Jesus' lips; and further comparative research will show that contemporary and earlier Jewish works offer much that goes to show the prevalence of an expectation of some catastrophe as is here set forth. At a later point[8] this chapter must form the subject of study, insofar as it relates to the concept of the Reign of God.

Assignments for Class Reports

1. In what other Gospels are to be found parallels to Mark 13? State any significant differences that you note.
2. How many parables are found in Mark, and where located?
3. After reading each parable carefully, give it the most descriptive title you can devise.

[7] The evangelist himself in his narrative, and upon the lips of others than Jesus, uses 107 additional words from the Old Testament. Of the 379 above, 78 Old Testament words of Jesus are in chapter 13. Outside chapter 13, 8.6 per cent of Jesus' words are from the Old Testament. Within chapter 13, 12.6 per cent of Jesus' words are from the Old Testament.

[8] Pages 61–64.

4. What language did Jesus probably speak? What words in this language are found in the second Gospel?
5. Point out instances in Mark where Jesus makes advantageous use of the question in teaching.
6. What constituted the Bible of the Christian Church at the time of the writing of our Gospel?
7. What explanation can you offer for the relatively large proportion of dialog in chapter 14?

Teaching of Jesus in Mark Addressed to the Twelve

Within the entire Gospel, Jesus addresses 2,132 words to the Twelve or to some of the disciples. Chapter 13 entire is addressed to disciples, verses 1f., the introduction, being a conversation with "one of his disciples," verses 3–37 being addressed to Peter, James, John, and Andrew. Taking the entire Gospel into consideration, about fifty-three per cent of Jesus' words in Mark are addressed to the Twelve or to some of their number.[9]

Because of the greater importance given to disciple instruction on the part of the Second Evangelist, the ethical material contained in this major part of Jesus' teaching according to Mark should first be studied.

The dialog material already mentioned need not be further examined. There are a number of passages clearly designed by the evangelist to give content to the intimate instruction of those men whom Jesus chose, "that they might be with him and that he might send them out to proclaim (the

[9] Without chapter 13, the percentage of Jesus' words addressed to the Twelve or some of their number shrinks to about 47 per cent.

Kingdom) and to have power to cast out demons."[10]

When the Master had carried the instruction of the Twelve to a certain point he sent them out upon a mission[11] involving a proclamation of the Reign of God, restoration of the mentally unsound to normal balance, and the teaching of such principles of the moral life as Jesus had already imparted to them.

In chapter 4 the evangelist sets forth some of the instruction preliminary to this mission, especially, verses 3–9, 11–20, 21–25.

The parable of the Different Soils is addressed to the "multitude," but verses 10ff. indicate that the parable was explained in private.[12] In their mission, and doubtless in later missions, the disciples would meet no constant degree of receptivity in their hearers. Many would fail to hear their message. But the recipients of the extensive private instruction of Jesus would be inducted into the "mysterion" of the Reign of God;[13] that is, they were to become familiar with its nature and its function in human affairs. The continued conversation reveals that not the Twelve alone were thus to become familiar with the real meaning of the Kingdom or Reign of God, but that all who hear with insight shall share in this knowledge.[14]

The explanation of the parable exhibits deep insight into the affairs of human life, which, indeed, enter practically into the development or inhibition

---

[10] Mark 3. 14. [11] 6. 7ff.

[12] Mark 4. 10 indicates that others besides the Twelve were present. But all are clearly disciples of Jesus. Luke understands that at least seventy besides the Twelve were sent on a public mission (Luke 10. 1).

[13] 4. 11a. [14] 4. 9, 21–25.

of the hearing, hence into the rise of that ability to hear with insight which characterizes those who know the Kingdom. The "fowls of the air," the "stony ground," "the sun," the "thorns" form a background to the picture in the parable which is plainly the background of life in its everyday aspect.

Had the reader access to this passage alone, the impression would readily be formed that the Twelve were fully aware of the nature of the Kingdom even when they went out to proclaim its coming;[15] but other items in the private instruction of the disciples show that the death of Jesus intervened before their knowledge became clear and unconfused, for Mark writes from such a later period that all early misunderstandings had been made plain.

The above discussion of Jesus' private explanation of his parable is somewhat enlightened by the evangelist's statement that this was but one of many parables that Jesus used in his public teaching[16] and that it was the custom of Jesus to speak only in parables to the multitude, while to his disciples he spoke more intimately in exposition.[17] But this statement of the evangelist is not to be taken to mean that Jesus never taught the people in any other form. Further study of Mark will reveal much that Jesus taught the people directly.

The second passage of importance to the teaching of the Twelve, according to Mark, is 7. 18–23. As before, the disciples ask the Master to explain what he had just declared in public. Jesus had come into conflict with Pharisees over ceremonial defilement.

---

[15] Mark 6. 7. [16] 4. 2. [17] 4. 33f.

They stressed the legal ablutions while Jesus had protested that defilement was not from without.[18] The disciples themselves were involved in the veiled charge of the Pharisees, hence their anxious question.[19] Jesus answered them:

> "Are you too thus without discernment? Do you not perceive that everything which proceeds into a man from outside is without power to defile him; that externals enter not into his heart, but into his digestive tract, and then pass off as waste?"

In the evangelist's view Jesus is here teaching an important ethical principle to his friends. The contamination to be dreaded is not that of the ritual, but that of the heart,[20] which is not so readily cleansed as mere bodily defilement. The sense of Jesus' words here clearly does not involve any conflict with a particular ceremonial law, and certainly the saying cannot be intended to do away with ritual distinctions, for such prevailed in the apostolic church,[21] but the Master's meaning is positive and affirmative. The moral life has its springs within, hence pure character is found where no inner source of spoiling exists. In modern terms, morality is based upon motives, the good will, personality itself; the Oriental teacher describes it intelligibly to his hearers by speaking of the heart in contrast to "outward" influences.

The third place to be considered is Mark 8. 15,

---

[18] Mark 7. 5–23. [19] 7. 17.

[20] "The heart," in Oriental phrase, means the essential inner person, the chief interests of a man, his "self," rather than the physical organ. See 1 Sam. 16. 7; Prov. 4. 23.

[21] See Acts 15. 20.

17b–21. After the feeding of the four thousand Jesus goes across the Sea of Galilee and the evangelist notes that the disciples had forgotten to take provisions with them. Thus when their Teacher begins to urge them to beware of the "leaven of the Pharisees and the leaven of Herod,"[22] they construe his words literally as a rebuke for their forgetfulness. Thereupon Jesus rebukes them indeed for their lack of insight, but does not offer them, as he had twice before, an explanation of his meaning.[23] They are left to find out for themselves, if they can, from Jesus' reference to the two miracles of feeding the multitude, what the Master means by those cutting words, "Do you not yet understand?"[24] The evangelist leads us to understand that Jesus' reference to the "leaven" means something essentially real and evil. The use of "leaven" in the New Testament, in fact, is almost altogether sinister, as witness parallels to Mark 8. 15, namely, Matt. 16. 6, 11; Luke 12. 1, and 1 Cor. 5. 7f.; Gal. 5. 9.

Most noteworthy is the fact that here for the fourth time[25] Jesus openly blames the disciples for their dullness. The evangelist utilizes the last unanswered question: "Do you not yet understand?" to leave with the reader the impression that the satisfaction of physical needs may so obsess a man as to obscure his moral vision. As far as the Gospels enlighten us, Jesus never put stress upon provision for bodily comfort or sustenance. But perhaps on many occasions the unenlightened disciple mind

---

[22] 8. 15. [23] See 4. 11–25 and 7. 18–23. [24] 8. 21b.

[25] 4. 13, 40; 7. 18 are the previous instances. Note also the implication of lack of understanding in 8. 4, compare 6. 37b, and recall the express statement of the evangelist, 6. 51f

thought one thing while Jesus meant something that had to do with higher planes of life.

The fourth significant instance of disciple instruction is found in Mark 8. 33, especially the words: "And he . . . rebuked Peter, with the words: Get behind me, Satan, for you are not thinking about the things of God but about the affairs of men."

In connection with Jesus' rebuke of Peter, there are three highly significant statements made by Jesus to his disciples. These can best be set forth in parallel columns.

Mark 8. 30	9. 31	10. 33–34
And he began to teach them that the Son of man must suffer many things, and must be rejected by the elders and by the chief priests and the scribes, and be killed, and after three days must rise again.	For he was teaching his disciples, and kept saying to them, The Son of man is delivered up into the hands of men, and they shall kill him; and although killed, after three days he shall rise again.	Lo, we are going up to Jerusalem; and the Son of man shall be delivered to the chief priests and the scribes; and they shall condemn him to death, and shall hand him over to the Gentiles, and they shall mock him, and spit upon him, and scourge him, and kill him; and after three days he shall rise again.

The first column introduces this note into the second Gospel. At this point in the story, at Cæsarea Philippi, just before the last journey to Jerusalem, Jesus undertook to show his disciples what kind of a Messiah he really was.

The second column contains the evangelist's explanation of Jesus' haste in passing through Galilee without the knowledge of the people,[26] and

[26] 9. 30.

is followed by the statement that the disciples did not understand Jesus' words and feared to ask again, probably dreading the rebuke the question would call forth.

The third column is in close connection with a statement[27] that the Twelve were greatly perplexed at the unusual bearing of their Master.

The teaching of these portions of Mark should be approached from the point of view of the writer. His generation understood the magnificent self-sacrifice of Jesus and its moral lesson. Even in Nero's day there were Christian martyrs who thoroughly experienced for themselves a devotion to truth unshaken by the presence of death. Whatever the historical event had proved, however, in the sixties, as to the Messiahship of Jesus, our evangelist teaches that the contemporaries of Jesus learned the real lesson of his life only after his death. Mark teaches others, in the words of Jesus, that the Master was offering in his life and death an exposition of his own teaching as to personal service and loyalty to principle. "If anyone will be first, he shall be last of all and servant of all." "Whoever would become great among you shall be your servant, . . . for even the Son of man did not come to be served but to serve, and to give his life a ransom for many."

The fifth instance of confidential address to the Twelve is offered in Mark 9. 29. Although brief, it is of considerable ethical significance, implying some progress, if slow, on the part of the disciples in the use of remedial methods. As a part of their commission[28] the Twelve had been given "authority

[27] 10. 32. [28] Mark 6. 7.

over unclean spirits." Their appeal to Jesus in the case of a lad who was dumb implies that in other cases they had successfully used this "authority." "Why could not we cast it out?" they asked,[29] with the emphasis upon "we." Jesus responded, "This sort cannot come out in any way except in prayer."

If, as appears quite certain, the men of Jesus' time thought often in terms of magic and often saw works of magic performed, it may be that the disciples had mistaken the giving of the "authority over unclean spirits" for the vital personal relation which all the evangelists emphasize as a *sine qua non* of efficient discipleship. The answer of Jesus is to be understood as encouragement rather than rebuke. As a true Teacher he patiently pointed out to these first disciples the lessons which, in the evangelist's day, had become standard Christian teaching.

Assignments for Class Reports

1. Make a list of the names of the Twelve, as found in the first three Gospels. Note differences in order and in names.
2. Read Mark 6. 7–13 and note whether Mark indicates any limits for the mission of the Twelve. Compare Matt. 10 and comment upon any new material found there or elsewhere in the first Gospel.
3. Paraphrase Mark 4. 10–25.
4. What is the Old Testament source for the teaching as to "defilement" to which the Pharisees refer in Mark 7. 5?
5. What traces of popular superstition can be found in such places as Mark 5. 28; 7. 35; Luke 13. 16; Matt. 12. 43–45? Consult Deissmann: *Light from the Ancient East*, pp. 302ff.

[29] 9. 28b.

6. Point out upon the map relative locations of Cæsarea Philippi, Sea of Galilee, Jerusalem.

TEACHING OF JESUS IN MARK ADDRESSED TO THE TWELVE (Concluded)

The sixth instance of address to the Twelve involves a lengthy portion of the ninth chapter. Verses 9.33b, 35b, 37 form Mark's version of one of the most important of Jesus' deliverances. Its ethical content does not demand ingenious apparatus for its formulation. These words set forth the demand of Jesus that his true followers show consideration for the rights and for the means of self-realization of others rather than seek their own advantage or press their own rights.

The misapprehension of the disciples as to the nature of the Kingdom of God, whose near approach Jesus and they themselves had heralded,[30] led them to suppose that there would be desirable places for them within that new order. But of the Twelve, who should precede? This occasioned an actual dispute among them. After the favorite Markan method, Jesus begins the lesson with a question: "What were you talking about as you came along?"

To this the disciples made no answer, whereupon Jesus reveals his knowledge of their selfish questionings and announces the principle which should have governed their thought about the Kingdom:

> "No man can push his way to prominence in the Kingdom of God; but, rather, if he desire prominence, let him show proficiency in serving, even if he appear to be last of all."[31]

[30] See 9. 1, "Some . . . shall not die till they see the Kingdom of God come in power."
[31] Mark 9. 35b.

This lesson of altruism and unselfishness was picturesquely enforced when Jesus reached for a near-by child and stood him before the Twelve as he told them that any service to the very least and most dependent was service rendered to their Master and to Him who sent Jesus into the world. Thus, not only their Teacher, who was now so well known to them, but God himself was included in the world of persons to whom service was due.[32]

The introduction of 9.39–50 in such immediate connection with the preceding words of Jesus,[33] indicates the evangelist's view that from verse 33 to verse 50 the discourse is unitary.[34]

The pericope[35] falls naturally into three portions:

First, 9.38–42. John's report that the disciples had forbidden an unknown miracle-worker to use the name of Jesus elicits the statement that the use of Jesus' name commended the man, "for," said Jesus, "he who does not oppose me is for me." No act of service, "in the name of Christ," can be in vain. But the opposite of reward will accrue

[32] This service does not appear to be worship in the conventional sense, but personal service, often vicarious. That a reciprocal relation exists between the Father and the disciple is a teaching which Mark and the other evangelists make plain. Mark 11. 25; Matt. 25. 31ff. See also under Mark 11. 22–25, p. 74.

[33] 9. 33b, 35b, 37.

[34] A glance at the parallel arrangement of the Gospels in any "harmony" reveals that Matthew and Luke dispose portions of this long Markan passage otherwise. No modern student can know in what order or in what context these words originally stood. But the task of the student is first of all, without question as to the original order or context, to approach the words as they stand. For here they represent either the understanding of the writer as to the original form and setting or they reflect his purpose with regard to the reader. Each evangelist clearly felt free to use discourse or narrative material in any order or context that best fitted his aim.

[35] 9. 38–50.

to anyone who puts obstacles in the way of any disciples, who, like children, are learning to walk, but easily fall.

Second, 9. 43–49. This suggests some causes for stumbling.[36] These may be found close at hand. Better remove any such cause than actually make a misstep. The test will surely come. So sacrifice even a bodily member rather than sacrifice life.

Third, 9.50. Personal character, after all, is the prize. As only salt with its own salty character is of worth, so only a person with his own personal values unmixed with base things is worthy. The verse is a clear statement, in its context, of the supreme good that resides in well developed character.

Between these three divisions of 9.38–50 there appear to be certain connectives. The phrase "cause one of these little ones to stumble" (42) suggests the "cause thee to stumble" (43). Again, the "salted with fire" (49) suggests the salt logion (50). Some divide between verses 48 and 49, thus placing the entire statement about salting with fire and having salt within oneself in one paragraph. But the "for" which introduces verse 49 makes it preferable to bind that verse closely with 43–48. Verse 50b stands alone, and in this form it is found in the writing of no other evangelist.[37]

The entire pericope, 9.39–50, has a real connection with the incident of the child, 9.35–37, as shown in the expression (42) "one of these little ones that

---

[36] The Greek word translated in some versions "offend" means "stumble."

[37] See Mark 9. 50a and Luke 14. 34.

believe on me," for in each case Jesus has in mind the attitude of men toward all who are in need of sympathy and help, and who may easily be imperiled in their progress.

What, then, is the teaching of the entire section, 9.39–50? Most interpreters admit that the meaning by no means lies plainly upon the surface, particularly in the latter part, containing enigmatical reference to salt and fire.

One must proceed as though only the Gospel of Mark were at hand in the interpretation of this particular portion of his writing. One must also keep in mind the preceding incident, 9. 33–37, for Jesus is represented as addressing these very disciples, one of whom admitted that he interfered with a man who was invoking Jesus' name, as he supposed, in an unwarranted way. Jesus, it will be recalled, defended the unknown man.

Further, it should be kept in mind that in the view of Mark, the Twelve were none too keen of insight. Thus it is not *prima facie* probable that the evangelist would represent to his original readers that Jesus spoke to these disciples in riddles, or in farfetched and intricate figures. Mark understands[38] that Jesus imparted the "secret" of the Kingdom, as plainly as he could, to the Twelve.

Again, the context shows[39] that the disciples needed instruction to correct their selfish ambition for place, and in 9.38ff. the evangelist shows further that the group was inclined selfishly to prevent others even from doing good in the name of their Master, for, said John, "he followed not us." This

---

[38] 4. 11. [39] 9. 35.

display of narrowness of spirit led Jesus to return to the thought of service. The unknown man was a servant of the good, and the disciple who hindered him was much like one who puts obstacles in the way of any believer. This is a serious offense.[40] The figure of sacrifice, whether of hand or foot or eye, or of any part or function that would, if retained, lead to the commission of any offense, is used by Mark as an exhortation to the Twelve to seek the highest moral values and the best ethical attitude at any expense, even the loss of something that is in itself good.

That Jesus considered that it would be literally necessary for any follower to amputate a member of his body in order acceptably to serve God is scarcely credible. As far as is known, none of them did resort to such measures.[41]

The Oriental teacher, Jesus, is being sketched here for a circle of Roman readers, primarily, and these readers had enough imagination to understand Jesus' figures better than many a modern commentator.

Thus the reader of to-day, putting himself into the place of an original reader of the Gospel, need not follow too literally the quotation[42] from Isa. 66. 24, but may accept it as Oriental imagery which a Palestinian teacher would naturally use. When Mark chose to place in this connection, then, the saying, "for everyone shall be salted with fire," the thought that he intended to convey to the

[40] 9. 42.
[41] The history of attempts on the part of later Christians to mutilate themselves sufficiently refutes a literal acceptance of these words of Jesus.
[42] 9. 48.

reader was that, as the Levitical ritual required that all sacrifices be salted,[43] and as the covenant relations between the Israelites and God were termed a "covenant of salt."[44] so in the new moral and social order the term "salt" stood for an essential element in the moral-spiritual life. "Have salt in yourselves!" as an exhortation, means, in this context, "Have the Kingdom-nature, which is the Father-nature, within you!" Peaceable relations between men who have "salt within themselves" are normal relations for the Kingdom.[45]

The expression, "for everyone shall be salted with fire" constitutes a difficulty in interpreting this address of Jesus, but it offers less difficulty if construed, as noted above, directly with the thought of verse 48. It partakes of the highly figurative nature of verse 48 and must apply to every person who "enters into the Kingdom of God"[46] that is, into the "life" spoken of in verses 43, 45. As an expression coined either by Jesus or by the evangelist, it expresses the thought that the hour of testing must come, that dicipleship is not a matter of form, and that the experience of him who qualifies would be well described as being made fit through sacrificial fire.

The seventh portion of the second Gospel in which are encountered instructive words of Jesus spoken to the disciples is 10.23b–25, 27bc, 29–31. These words constitute the succeeding context to the narrative of the Rich Young Ruler, as he is often

[43] Lev. 2. 13. [44] Num. 18. 19.
[45] The student is referred to the Sermon on the Mount and to Matt. 18 for the clearest expression in the gospel literature of this idea.
[46] Mark 9. 47.

termed. Mark does not tell us that he was young, but that he had observed the law from youth up. It is not said in any Gospel that he was a ruler, although he was a well-instructed man and evidently averaged well in his practice of the excellent moral instruction he had received. The man was indeed rich, a characteristic essential for the sequel, although the reader is not informed as to the nature of his wealth.

His inquiry was, "How can I inherit eternal life?"[47] Jesus began with the law, which assuredly the man would know. When the inquiry went beyond the contemporary synagogue teaching, Jesus made a very concrete and specific proposal, "Supply your essential deficiency; go sell whatever you have and give to the poor, and you will have treasure in heaven; also come and follow me."[48]

The refusal of the rich man to accept this proposal had a sobering and disappointing effect upon the Teacher. With pathos he turned to his disciples and lamented: "With what difficulty shall they that have riches enter into the Kingdom of God!"

Thus far, it appears, the disciples shared the emotion of Jesus, although they indicated some lack of understanding of the whole incident. Jesus repeated and further illustrated his comment:

> "Children, how difficult it is to enter into the Kingdom of God! It is easier for a camel to pass through a needle's eye than for a rich man to enter into the Kingdom of God."[49]

The use of the vocative, "Children," betrays the Teacher's solicitude for those before him.

---

[47] 10. 17b. [48] 10. 21. [49] 10. 24b, 25.

After the exchange of expressions of astonishment at this saying, Peter[50] calls attention to the renunciation practiced by the Twelve, in that they left all to follow Jesus. With the rich man's question[51] in mind, Jesus declared that such renunciation brings its rewards, both present and future. Persecutions are promised along with whatever material advantage may accrue, "and in the coming age eternal life."[52] The following sentence, which forms the conclusion of this address of Jesus, is cryptic enough: "Many first shall be last, and many last shall be first."[53]

Interpreting this statement in its present position, without reference to other uses made of it, the relative attitudes of the rich man who has just departed after his refusal to accept Jesus' proposal and of the disciples, who had given up all to follow Jesus, are contrasted. The contemporary order of things and that new order taught by Jesus under the name of "the Kingdom of God" are also in contrast. The rich occupy first places in this order, but their very riches tend to prevent them from being first in that order where personal values, character, "treasures in heaven" are the things that qualify one for chief place. These words constitute a very solemn closing of an important message to the disciples. Well may they have profited by its confidential and warning tone.

No one can justly find in this pericope any condemnation of wealth as such. The influence of the

[50] 10. 28. [51] 10. 17b. [52] 10. 29–31.

[53] Weizsäcker: Text-bibel, translates very accurately the thought, "Vielmal, aber, werden die ersten die letzten sein und die letzten die ersten" (Mark 10. 31).

possession of wealth upon personality is emphasized. As far as moral achievement is concerned, Jesus says, as Mark puts it, that the possession of wealth constitutes a real peril. A rich man may too readily accept the primacy given him by his contemporaries, not perceiving its superficial character. On the other hand, mere renunciation in itself may bring no moral advantage. But renunciation for the sake of some high end, such as service of one's fellow men, is actually enriching, bringing wealth in terms of character.

The eighth portion to be examined is the evangelist's report of an intimate conversation between Jesus and his disciples, James and John, the two sons of Zebedee, whom Jesus had early called to follow him.[54] The reference is Mark 10. 36, 38, 39b–40, 42–45. James and John preferred an ambitious request[55] concerning places of influence for themselves in the "glory" of Jesus, doubtless influenced by a wrong conception of the Kingdom of God which Jesus had said was soon to come.[56] The human nature in the whole proceeding is well portrayed, and its exposition lies on the surface.

The ten who were not taken into the counsel of James and John became angry with the two, thereby improving the situation in no way. It was a real emergency in the training of the Twelve, and Mark uses the opportunity of setting forth Jesus' teaching as to the high value of service to one another in the Kingdom. The teaching is not new but it is set forth in new terms.

First, Jesus called the two ambitious disciples to

---

[54] Mark 1. 19f. [55] 10. 37. [56] 9. 1.

him, and afterward the ten. Each group had its own lesson. Jesus showed the two their appropriate privileges as his disciples to drink the cup and to be baptized with the baptism that was his. This the two voluntarily accepted, whereupon Jesus called the ten, and patiently reiterated the lesson of 9.35 in the words:

> "You know that those who seem to rule the Gentiles bear themselves as their lords, and their great ones use their authority oppressively over them. Not thus is it among you; but whoever wills to become great among you shall be your servant, and whoever wills to become chief among you shall be slave of all; for even the Son of man did not come to be served but to serve, and to give his life a ransom for many." 10. 42b–45.[57]

The ninth instance of address to the Twelve appears in 12. 43–44, following the story of the widow who bestowed her gift of two mites in the Temple treasury. Jesus' words of commendation were scarcely heard by the poor widow, but Mark has incorporated them in his account of Jesus' words as follows:

> "Truly I tell you that this poor widow put in more than all those who are putting money into the treasure chest; for all put in from their abundance, but from her lack, this woman put in all that she had, all her support."[58]

Here the poor, not the rich, has the center of the stage. The rich man of 10.21 was required to give

[57] Deissmann's note on the Greek word 'lutron,' ransom, in *Light from the Ancient East*, pp. 331–2, should be consulted.

[58] 12. 43b–44.

much, this widow gave pitifully little, but she went down to her house justified rather than the rich man, who, no doubt, really desired eternal life. Mark lays great stress upon the lesson of sacrifice, as this short address bears witness. In his own person Jesus taught that "to serve and to give his life a redemption price for many" (as it may properly be phrased), is both highest duty and greatest good.

The tenth and last passage containing words of Jesus of ethical import addressed to the disciples is found in Mark 14. 6–9.[59] The pericope contains brief but striking statements, the text of the discourse being furnished by a woman who lavished expensive perfume upon Jesus himself. Whether impressed by the words, "Give to the poor and thou shalt have treasure in heaven,"[60] by some other words which required of the disciple unselfish devotion, or even by words so recently spoken,[61] "The Son of man did not come to be served," "some" who stood by sought to restrain the woman from her deed. Mark does not say that these were disciples, but the inference from later narratives is that Jesus' words here were addressed to the Twelve.[62] Judas was present, according to Mark 14. 10, and the "some" are doubtless of the disciple group.

Jesus here for the first time accepts an act of service for himself. Three times, at least, he taught his disciples that he was on his way to suffering and death, as he took his way toward Jerusalem. Now he is in Jerusalem (or in Bethany, on

[59] 13. 5b–37 consists of an eschatological discourse, the longest on Jesus' lips in this Gospel. It is addressed to four disciples, but because of its peculiar nature, the chapter will be discussed under another rubric. See page 61ff.

[60] 10. 21b. [61] 10. 45. [62] Matt. 26. 8; John 12. 4.

the Mount of Olives) and his fate appears imminent. But his followers seem to think rather of a triumphal march to a new economic or political order[63] than of death for their leader. One woman seems to have taken him literally. Lest she be unable to perform the last tender rites for the beloved dead when his fate should overtake him, she bestows her rich gift of love even while he is at supper. Jesus indicates his appreciation of this attitude in the words, "She did what she could; she anticipated the anointing of my body for burial."[64]

It is not to be assumed that this woman of literal faith perceived coming events in detail. Her belief in his own words[65] prompted the timely service. The celebration of her deed in coming generations[66] would not be for the cost of the perfume, over which "some" grieved, but for the sympathetic response of her soul to the self-sacrifice of her Master. The material values shrink in Jesus' thought before those eternal values of a developing personality.

The foregoing ten selections from Jesus' addresses to his immediate disciples contain the important private ethical teaching of the Master as Mark presents it. Other passages might have been adduced, as the instructions[67] to the disciples as they went on their mission; the remark,[68] evidently addressed to the Twelve, "O faithless generation!"; an explanation in private of Jesus' view of remarriage after divorce,[69] and the prophecy of Peter's denial,[70] which is not so much teaching but serves chiefly in imparting dramatic force to the narrative.[71]

[63] 9. 34; 10. 37; 11. 7-10. [64] 14. 8. [65] For example, 8. 30f.; 9. 31bc; 10. 33. [66] 14. 9. [67] 6. 8–11. [68] 9. 19. [69] 10. 11b, 12. [70] 14. 30f.

[71] Mark does what no other Gospel writer did in noting (14. 68c) the first cock-crow just before the second denial of Peter.

The words of Jesus spoken in the garden direct the disciples as to their personal bearing in the approaching crisis, but furnish no element of specific ethical instruction, except by implication. With the anointing of Jesus' body in anticipation of his burial and the Master's comment upon the act, Mark ceases to introduce examples of formal instruction to the Twelve.

At this point a summary of the ethical teaching of the Twelve by Jesus as the Second Evangelist presents it, finds appropriate place.

The phrase "Kingdom of God" appears frequently upon Jesus' lips. In contemporary thought the term "Reign of God" doubtless best expressed the original Aramaic phrase. Jesus nowhere defines his understanding of the term, but the ambitious request of the two disciples[72] and Jesus' answer leave no doubt that something other than a merely political or economic order was in his mind. The announcements of his passion prepare the reader for the sequel, which makes it impossible for Jesus to rule in person over the new order. Conventional standards of preeminence within the Kingdom are apparently reversed.[73]

Wealth, like other impersonal values, may prove a hindrance to one who desires to be under the Reign of God. But this hindrance is found in the use of the material thing and in the interest or affection lavished upon it. Personal values, on the other hand, reckoned in terms of service and character, rank high among those who find place in the new order.

Jesus' teaching in these respects evidently departed from the contemporary synagogue instruction,

[72] 10. 35ff. [73] 9. 35b.

for the disciples were slow in apprehending their Master's meaning. Even in the exercise of efficient prayer these men were unskillful,[74] although they must have prayed after the Jewish manner all their lives.

Altruism and unselfishness stand out as chief elements in character that is approved for entrance into the Kingdom. This chief note in the private instruction of Jesus was reinforced by the example of the Teacher himself.

Assignments for Class Reports

1. Upon examination of the context, show whether Mark understands that 4. 21–34 represents private or public instruction. If addressed to the Twelve, what elements could be added to the foregoing summary?
2. What evidence is to be found in the teaching considered above that Jesus had little or no interest in human life as it is actually lived? What evidence is found to the contrary?
3. Is there any good reason for supposing that the poor were more responsive to Jesus' teaching than were the rich? Can you offer any evidence that the situation is now changed in this respect?
4. Find the essential features in the Pharisees' teaching as to the Kingdom of God in Jesus' time.
5. Paraphrase the story of the woman who anointed Jesus' head with perfume. Bring out the ethical features of the narrative clearly.
6. Present your own understanding of "the greatest good" or *summum bonum*, in Jesus' ethical teaching according to Mark, thus far.

Popular Addresses and Parables

Mark makes it clear that Jesus taught in public

[74] 9. 29.

and that his favorite method was the use of simile or parable, many of which were employed but few of which the evangelist records. The parable of 12. 1–11 is addressed to the religious leaders, according to the demand of the context, although the people may have overheard it.

Mark does not consistently maintain that Jesus spoke only in parables to the people,[75] for while 218 Greek words suffice for his report of the parables in Mark 4. 3–9, 26–32, there are 311 Greek words used to report words that Jesus addresses to the "multitudes," as Mark picturesquely puts it, in 1.15; 3.33–35; 6.4; 8.34b–9. 1; 12.35b–37a, and 12. 38–40; to which may be added words addressed to a foreign woman, namely, 7. 27, 29.

The study of this popular teaching throws further light upon the concept of the Kingdom of God. It cannot be presumed, however, that this teaching was as clearly apprehended by Jesus' hearers as by the readers of the second Gospel. The following paragraphs present the gist of this popular teaching in Mark.

Mark 1. 14f.:

> "After the arrest of John, Jesus came into Galilee proclaiming the good news of God in the words: The time is fulfilled and the Reign of God draws nigh: Repent and believe in the good news."

In this public proclamation, Jesus assumes an expectation of the coming of a new era. The time of acceptation is ripe, the new era is at hand. Naturally, the hearers want to know how to enjoy the

---

[75] 4. 34.

privileges of the new order. Two conditions, "repentance" and "faith," are to be met.[76]

The saying has more ethical meaning than theological. It is addressed to men not versed in the lore of the scribes but, rather, too well versed in the oppressive conditions of the life they live. Both conditions, repentance and faith, have to do with conduct, but conduct, in Jesus' thought, is not merely mechanical behavior. Conduct, with the Teacher, is behavior produced by the life itself, by underlying nature and motive. Thus, repentance involves a change of attitude, a renewed thought about God and men; while faith, holding here much of its Old Testament sense, means a practical dependence upon and cooperation in the new order as an acknowledgment of the presence of God in the world of human persons.

Mark 3. 33-35 constitutes words addressed to the public in the form of an excursus or interjection. Jesus was teaching a large crowd that sat about him[77] when word was brought that his mother and his brothers were outside, asking for him:

> "And in answer to them he said, Who is my mother and my brothers? and after surveying those seated about him in a circle, he said: Behold my mother and my brothers; whosoever does the will of God, the same is my brother and sister and mother."

It cannot be an accident that Mark introduced these words thus early in his narrative, for they explain that the relation of the disciple to the Master

---

[76] A. B. Bruce: *The Kingdom of God*, pp. 94-108, argues cogently that faith is in reality the sole basis of entrance to the Kingdom.

[77] 3. 32.

accounts for the successful "repentance" and "belief" which admit to the Kingdom. The relationships indicated in the terms "mother," "sister," "brother," are such as involve likeness of nature.[78] Mark considered the saying so significant that he omitted all other discourse of Jesus on that occasion and preserved only this ejaculation.

Mark 6. 4 contains an impulsive retort of Jesus, perhaps in itself a proverbial expression. The scene is the synagogue at Nazareth and Jesus is addressing his fellow townsmen. They do not accept him as a teacher, whereupon he exclaims: "A prophet is not unappreciated except in his homeland and among his relatives and in his city."

Mark had already shown[79] that Jesus' family tried to restrain him from teaching, and in this place it appears that no "faith" or practical dependence upon him as a teacher existed in his homeland, not enough even to enable him to work cures, except upon the very few.[80]

The evangelist indicates that the element of faith in Jesus conditioned the success of his program, as surely as faith was a condition of entrance into the Kingdom of God which Jesus taught was imminent.

Mark 7. 27, 29 presents two interesting statements of Jesus made to a woman not an Israelite. She begged healing for her daughter:

> "First let the children be satisfied," said Jesus; "it is not seemly to take the bread of the children and throw it to the curs." The woman responded with the words: "Yes, Mas-

---

[78] This saying is very important, as will be seen in its further exposition on page 71f.

[79] 3. 21. [80] 6. 5.

ter, even the curs under the table are accustomed to eat of the children's crumbs."

The significance attached to these words by the evangelist is seen in the further reply of Jesus: "Because of this answer depart, the demon has gone out of your daughter."

If faith is evidenced by activity, coupled with strategy and wit, this woman had qualified as a recipient of God's good gifts. Jesus found her spirit a congenial one, unlike those of his native city. Mark admits that a person not an Israelite received good at Jesus' hands. The admission goes further, however. It teaches that others than Israelites, in the thought of Jesus, may obtain good things through faith in him and in God, as well as can the descendants of Abraham. In this incident the evangelist has taught the fundamental truth of that universalism which, in the view of the first evangelist, Jesus himself did not teach.[81]

Mark 8. 34b–9. 1 constitutes the longest address to the people to be found in the second Gospel, only the parable of the Soils and the two parables of the Inevitable Fruitage and of the Mustard Seed in chapter 4 approaching this passage in length.[82]

Jesus called the crowd to him, with his disciples, and thus addressed them all:

---

[81] "Universalism" is here used to mean the world-wide, international application of Jesus' teaching, as, for example, Paul practiced it. Compare Matt. 15. 21–28. The First Evangelist does not admit that Jesus went into a house in heathen territory (compare Mark 7. 24), nor even that Jesus went into that land (see Matt. 15. 22), but to its borders. See Matt. 10. 5f.; 15. 24 for nationalistic sentiment.

[82] There are one hundred and twenty-two Greek words in 8. 34b–9. 1; one hundred and thirteen in Mark 4. 26–32, and one hundred and five in 4. 3–9.

"If any one decides to come after me, (that is, be my disciple), let him deny himself and let him take up his cross and follow me. For whosoever sets his mind upon his own life shall lose it, but whosoever shall lose his life for the sake of the glad tidings, (that is, the proclamation concerning the Reign of God), shall save it. For what profits it a man to gain the whole world and to lose his life? for what should a man give as a ransom for his life? For whosoever is ashamed of me and of my words in this immoral and sinful generation, of him also shall the Son of man be ashamed, when he shall come in the glory of his Father, with the holy angels." And he said to them, "Verily I tell you that there are certain of those who stand here who shall not taste of death until they see the Reign of God having come in power."

The last part of this address possesses elements which relate it to chapter 13. For the present, attention will not be fixed upon this part of the evangelist's message. The first part of the pericope, however, distinctly contributes to the ethical program of Jesus in this Gospel.

Some men have probably offered themselves as disciples of Jesus, attracted by his announcement that the Reign of God is at hand. The time is late in Jesus' ministry. A major turning-point in his career has just been reached. If the Master takes his mission seriously, so must the disciple. To follow Jesus is to do the will of God, as Jesus does. To be his disciple is to enter upon the supreme moral adventure of life. But moral enterprises have great risks. Did not the prophets lay down their lives for their convictions? Truly, asserts Jesus, a man who decides to follow him must be ready to lose his life, for, strangely yet truly enough, if one decides to save one's life at all hazards, then one will achieve less in the moral realm. The attention will be fixed upon conservation of physical existence. Then how can due attention be placed upon character development, upon spiritual achievement? Like the Master, the follower must make the physical life subordinate to the supreme demand of truth, of loyalty, of the life of the soul itself.

The address of Jesus here is in the nature of a challenge. But it is based upon such considerations as were familiar to all who heard. In no place has any evangelist made a sharper contrast between material values and personal worth.

Mark 12. 35b–37a. These verses present a Messianic riddle, ostensibly addressed to the people, but not answered by anyone:[83]

> "How say the scribes that Christ is the son of David? David himself said, in the Holy Spirit, The Lord said to my lord, Sit on my right hand until I put thine enemies under thy feet. David himself calls him lord, whence then is he his son?"

The remark of the evangelist immediately following this unanswered question of Jesus, that the people heard with enjoyment, indicates to the reader that the scribes, who were no popular favor-

[83] This may be a part of the address to the scribe of 12. 28, for the phrase "and the great crowd was hearing him gladly" (12. 37b), could belong to the following paragraph. But the question (35b), "How say the scribes . . . ?" implies that Jesus was addressing the laity and having a little fun in exposing their dilemma.

ites, were victims of the wit of their Teacher. It is, of course, known to Bible students of to-day that David did not write the one hundred and tenth psalm, from which the quotation is made. To Jesus' contemporaries, however, this was not known, and the argument must be accepted upon that basis. In any event, the dilemma is in the speculative and not in the practical realm, thus contributes little if anything to an investigation into the moral precepts of Jesus.

Mark 12. 38–40 almost immediately follows the Messianic riddle, and, indeed, may, in the thought of the writer, be a continuation of the discourse in the Temple. The words were uttered "in the course of his teaching," larger portions of which are preserved by the other synoptic writers. These words of Mark contain very serious charges against the scribes:

> "Beware of the scribes, who desire to walk about in long robes and seek greetings in the market places and chief seats in the synagogues, and high places at feasts, who devour the houses of widows and who for appearance's sake say long prayers. These shall receive greater judgment."

Mark's original readers were probably members of the church in the city of Rome. Mark, however, had earlier lived in Jerusalem, and his own mother may have known instances of such immorality on the part of the scribes. But in Rome, also, there is every reason to suppose, there existed such instances of hypocrisy as here set forth. Such men, wherever found, represent a moral antinomy. Matthew, who wrote for Palestinian readers, expanded this address in the temple into a most cutting denunciation of the religious leaders.[84] But Mark does not appear to include all the scribes in his denunciation, for within a few verses,[85] he has Jesus tell a scribe that he is "not far from the Reign of God."

No one may plead position or influence as an excuse for moral turpitude or for immoral deeds, declares the Master. Jesus saw that the existing religious institutions were losing caste morally, while emphasizing formal religious observances. The emphasis upon moral uprightness, correspondence of inner motive and outer act, comes well at the close of Mark's record of Jesus' popular teaching.

In the foregoing exposition of popular address the few parables addressed to the people have been omitted. At this point some consideration must be given them.

Of the three parables in chapter four, the second and third are introduced by the formulas, "Thus is the Kingdom of God"[86] and "How shall we liken the Kingdom of God, or in what simile shall we set it forth?"[87] With the first parable no such formula is used. The explanation of this parable of the different soils[88] was given in the presence of the Twelve, but the parable itself was spoken before a great crowd on the shore of the Sea of Galilee.[89] As the discussion above[90] has shown, this is not so much a kingdom-parable as it is a graphic portrayal of the different degrees of success with which the Twelve will meet in their mission. But so funda-

---

[84] Matt. 23. Consult Burton and Goodspeed, *A Harmony of the Synoptic Gospels.*

[85] 12. 34. [86] 4. 26. [87] 4. 30.

[88] Note the title of this parable in Burton and Goodspeed: *A Harmony of the Synoptic Gospels.*

[89] 4. 1. [90] See pages 22–23.

mental is the truth involved, so true to human nature, that all who are interested in social betterment and moral uplift find conditions analogous to these types of soil. Some hearers do not retain the message at all, some are superficial and enthusiastic but without endurance, some accept the truth but give it no open space to grow into their mental habit, when other interests obliterate it. But some hear, appropriate, and cultivate. Life is the fruitage.

Two parables that shed light upon the idea of the Reign of God are found in Mark 4. 26–29, 30–32. The first may be called "A Parable of Inevitable Fruitage," the second, usually called the parable of the Mustard Seed, may better be entitled "A Parable of Small Beginnings," "A Parable of Encouragement."

The parable of Inevitable Fruitage is found only in this Gospel. It reads:

> "Thus is the Reign of God, as if a man should cast the seed upon the earth, and should sleep and arise, night and day, and the seed should sprout and grow to its height, how, he himself knows not. The earth brings forth of itself, first a green shoot, then an ear, then full grain in the ear. And when it yields a harvest, immediately he sends forth the sickle and the harvest becomes a fact."

The teaching of the parable is that fruitage is inevitable, granted proper conditions. Not the seed itself, but the life within the seed is emphasized. The earth brings forth "of itself" because of the inherent life in good seed. So the Kingdom has life in itself, which will inevitably bring its appropriate product. Stages in its growth must be noted, patience may be needed, but confidence in the outcome is the disciple's right.

As with all parables, every term in the simile may not be equally stressed. Here the sickle, for example, constitutes a part of the setting, not a prominent feature. A proper ending of an agricultural story includes the gathering of the grain. But in this parable the sickle cannot be invested with the significance that it has in another type of writing.[91] Verse 28 contains the gist of the parable and offers the point of emphasis: "The earth brings forth of itself, first a green shoot, then an ear, then full grain in the ear."

The verses immediately following the Parable of Inevitable Fruitage constitute a simile designed to show how the Kingdom of God may become exceedingly great, even with small beginnings. The Parable of Small Beginnings[92] reads thus:

> "How shall we liken the Kingdom of God, or in what simile shall we set it forth? As a mustard seed, which is smaller than all the seeds sown upon the earth, and when it is sown it grows up and becomes greater than all the herbs, and puts forth great branches, so that under its shadow the birds of the heavens can nest."

The disciples and others who heard these words were dwelling in the days of small things. The teaching is universally sound, however, that a program of truth will attract to itself more and more adherents. The worthy elements of life may at a

---

[91] For example, Revelation 14. 14f., 17ff.

[92] 4. 30–32.

given period seem pitifully small, but in the perspective of the ages the larger growth of the almost invisible germ must appear.

Some sense of fulfillment, even in his day, must have come to the evangelist. For, in his day, Paul had carried the new movement and its ethical program into the heart of the Roman Empire, even to the capital city. And in this very imperial city, Mark, looking back over the forty years, more or less, since the parables were uttered, must have been guided in his choice of these from so many[93] because the full grain was appearing to him to be forming in the ear, and the mustard plant was already spreading its branches[94].

The section on "Popular Address and Parables" of Jesus may be summarized thus:

Jesus spoke publicly of the Reign of God as imminent. The invitation to enjoy its privileges contained announcement of two conditions which must be fulfilled; first, the appropriate attitude must be attained (repentance); second, practical alliance with and dependence upon the movement as a program of individual and social betterment must follow (faith). Both conditions involve ethical values.

The new order was not to arrive suddenly, nor would it be fully developed at first. Like a seed, with life in it, it would reach maturity through nor-

[93] Mark 4. 2, 10b, 33.

[94] The assumption is made that these three parables of Mark 4 were spoken before a larger number of people than the Twelve. With the Parable of the Soils this is clear. With the other two the case stands thus: Mark assures us (4. 33f.) that parables were spoken in public even if explained in private. The words (4. 21, 24) "he said to them" most likely means the disciples. But (4. 26, 30) "And he said" seems to begin a different address, probably public.

mal stages, but its fruitage would come with full growth. Small beginnings could not discourage one who had faith in the vitality of the new order.

An ethical relation is established between the man who "does the will of God" and Jesus, who proclaims the coming Reign of God. The terms of family relation appropriately describe this brotherhood.

Membership in the community thus bound together by ethical attitude and relation is to be undertaken seriously. Loyalty to the new moral program may demand sacrifice of life itself.

Contemporary teachers of religion (scribes) may not be taken as standards of conduct, for often their religion is unethical. Among those engaged in the program of the Reign of God, the inner life and motive must be the effective spring of all action.

Assignments for Class Reports

1. What particulars, if any, does this chapter add to Mark's exposition of the Reign of God?
2. In your own words, explain the ethical content of "repentance" and "faith."
3. Collect evidence from this Gospel to show that Jesus' own family had little sympathy with his mission.
4. In what way does the narrative of the Greek woman of Mark 7. 26ff. illustrate the saying: "Seek and you shall find?" Where is this saying found?
5. Paraphrase Mark 8. 34-37.
6. Make a list of English words, new to you, found in the first four chapters of the textbook. Give their proper pronunciation and explain their meaning.
7. What was the origin and history of the scribes of Jesus' time?
8. By what means do various authorities designate the

parables of Mark 4? Criticize these titles, selecting those most descriptive.

Words Addressed to Contemporary Religious Leaders and Teachers

In thirteen places[95] within the second Gospel Jesus addresses some of the religious leaders and teachers directly, in a majority of the instances challenging them upon something that they had said, or upon their evident attitude. In three additional instances[96] the rulers in question probably overheard the words of Jesus.[97]

These addresses, involving 923 Greek words, are selected by Mark to exhibit the Master's appraisal of such moral leadership as Judaism enjoyed.

The distribution of these words throughout the Gospel is of interest. Six instances are found in chapters 2 and 3; seven are in chapters 11 and 12. The three remaining instances of direct or overheard address are found in chapters 7, 8, and 10, one in each chapter. Thus, at the beginning and at the end of the ministry of Jesus the Second Evangelist places the greatest conflict of Jesus with contemporary teachers and men of influence in his ancestral religion.

The questions involved are either ethico-religious or strictly ethical in character. Of the first type, the question as to the authority of Jesus to forgive sin,[98] to drive out the traders from the Temple,[99]

---

[95] 2. 8b–11; 2. 17bc; 2. 19–22; 2. 25b–28; 3. 4; 3. 23–29; 7. 6–13; 10. 3, 5–9; 11. 29f., 33b; 12. 1–11; 12. 15b, 16, 17b; 12. 24–27; 12. 29–31, 34.

[96] 8. 12b; 11. 17b; 12. 35b–37a.

[97] For example, 11. 18, "chief priests and scribes heard."

[98] 2. 10. [99] 11. 33.

or the demand for a sign from heaven to confirm his claim to divine authority,[100] the Messiah question raised by Jesus himself and not answered,[101] and again, early in his ministry[102] the cryptic words about a new ethico-religious order, and the right use of the Temple-area,[103] together with a speculative question about the rights of several husbands to one wife at the resurrection, constitute the substance.

Of the strictly ethical questions raised or answered by the Teacher, there are the following: Jesus asserted his authority in the moral field by pointing out to those who criticized him for consorting with social outcasts that these are in reality the needy. As such they have a prior claim upon one who can aid them.[104] Jesus charges that the established leaders have proved, on the whole, disloyal to their trust[105] and that many religious teachers of the day are superficial, even hypocritical.[106] He plainly answers a practical inquiry as to what constitutes the most important moral precept. The answer is in terms of the Torah[107] and plainly tells his questioner, when he shows some clear understanding of this precept, that he is "not far from the Kingdom of God."[108]

Early in his Gospel Mark put Jesus on record[109] as to the practical impossibility of divided allegiance. "If a house be divided against itself, that house cannot stand."[110] This practical observation is in the spirit of the Shema which the scribe recited[111]

[100] 8. 12b.
[101] 12. 37b–38a.
[102] 2. 19–22.
[103] 11. 17b.
[104] 2. 17b.
[105] 12. 1–11.
[106] 7. 6–13.
[107] 12. 29–31.
[108] 12. 34b.
[109] 3. 24.
[110] 3. 25.
[111] 12. 29ff.

and is again expressed in the answer of Jesus to a captious political question, "Cæsar's things render to Cæsar and God's things to God."[112]

Two other ethical problems raised in Jesus' discourse with the contemporary teachers concerned the observance of the Sabbath and the legality of divorce.

Jesus indicated[113] that the Sabbath as an institution should not lord it over human beings. Men should use the institution in the spirit of a helpful agency. Jesus argued that in time of need David, the great king, ate the sacred bread from before the altar. David's need surpassed the right even of a religious custom. Thus, Jesus ruled, any deed that was for the good of men might be performed on the Sabbath, custom to the contrary notwithstanding.[114] In the saying, "The Son of man is lord even of the Sabbath" he subordinated the letter of the law or any outgrown or unyielding institution to the demand for conservation of human values.

The divorce question must find place for fuller discussion in a later chapter, for the problem attracted the attention of each of the synoptic writers, and the tradition as to what Jesus really said reveals specific differences in Matthew, Mark and Luke. In the second Gospel,[115] in answer to an inquiry made probably by Pharisees,[116] Jesus criticized the Deuteronomic warrant for divorce,[117] asserting that marriage is essentially indissoluble. With his disciples privately[118] the Teacher discourses

---

[112] 12. 17. [113] 2. 25b–28; 3. 4. [114] 3. 4–6. [115] 10. 3, 5–9.
[116] The words "Pharisees, coming to him," are not certainly original.
[117] Deut. 24. 1–3. [118] 10. 11f.

further upon the implications of his public statement, especially with respect to remarriage after divorce.

The antipathy which Jesus revealed toward the teaching and the character of some of his contemporaries suggests the inquiry whether this attitude extended to the religion or moral teaching contained in their Scriptures. A brief investigation into the use of Old Testament quotations by the Second Evangelist will offer an answer.

Without reference to the 107 Greek words from the Old Testament used in the narrative by Mark or placed by him on the lips of others, there are 379 words on Jesus' lips which, according to the editors of the Westcott and Hort Greek Testament, are words from the Jewish Scriptures. Analysis of these words shows that 126 words, in ten quotations, are from the Torah; 196 words, in twenty-seven quotations, are from the prophets; while fifty-seven words are taken from the Psalms.

Practically all the quotations from the Torah are made with approval. The exceptions are Deut. 24. 1, quoted in Mark 10.4, and the law of the Levirate marriage, which Jesus comments upon, giving tacit approval to the law itself, but disapproving the Sadducees' use of it. The quotation, it should be noted, is not included among the words counted above as those of Jesus. Some of the quotations are not important, being rather formal likenesses, but the majority are easily identified as words taken intentionally from the Scriptures.

The preponderance of quotations from the prophets, Isaiah being the favorite, with nine quotations; Daniel, with six; Ezekiel, with three; Zechariah, with three; Malachi and Joel, two each; Micah and Jeremiah, one each, is noticeable. As far as the great preachers of righteousness of the past are concerned, Jesus has no criticism. The divorce law may have served in its time, but had become antiquated. But in their great declarations as to the duty and good of men the law and the prophets were authoritative.

In matters of ritual, it seems probable that Jesus was precise, if the detail involved did not collide with human need or with any personal prerogative. The leper[119] Jesus told to go and show himself to the priest, for Lev. 14. 2ff. required the priest to act as health officer for the community in such cases. Yet, when a hard-and-fast Sabbath rule, drawn up by the predecessors of the contemporary teachers, would deny to a needy man a deed of mercy,[120] or to hungry men available food, Jesus set forth his protest that "the Sabbath was made for man."[121] In such manner the great Teacher sets personal values higher than venerable institutions and even traditional codes.

Jesus is clear that the prophets had deep and accurate insight into moral problems and a high appraisal of personal values. When Jesus cleanses the Temple he appeals to the words of Isa. 56. 7, "My house shall be called a house of prayer for all peoples." And even before the time of that Temple of which the prophet of Isa. 56.7 spoke, Jeremiah had said that the Temple had become a "den of robbers."[122]

That the prophets placed obedience before sac-

---

[119] 1. 44. [120] For example, 2. 25–28; 3. 3b–5. [121] 2. 27.
[122] Jer. 7. 11.

rifice, and a right life before formal offerings to God, Jesus acknowledged in his words of appreciation of that scribe[123] who quoted the essence of Mic. 6. 6–8. That scribe was not far from the Kingdom which Jesus was announcing as imminent.

In summarizing this study of Jesus' words to contemporary religious leaders and teachers, and his attitude toward the moral instruction which their Scriptures and institutions represented, it must be admitted that the Master did not turn abruptly away from the current ethics. There was much that was sound and permanent in the teachings of those who had gone before him. This worthy heritage he sought to bring out in its full value. He put emphasis where it seemed to him appropriate, he placed old statements in new perspective, but at the same time he stigmatized as false prophets all who deliberately obscured ancient truth. The casuistry of the day[124] he scored in the very words of the prophet[125] who rebuked his contemporaries for drawing near to God with their lips and actually (in their hearts) remaining far from him.

That all human values were not clearly comprehended in the law was evident to Jesus. When the rich man declared that he had kept all the commandments in the Decalog[126] there was "one thing" still lacking. He must find a vital and sympathetic fellowship with men who were hungry for more than food and poor in other than money. Between these men and him the barrier was wealth. Yet even the Old Testament prophets understood some of these higher ethical values, as when Isaiah

[123] Mark 12. 32. [124] Mark 7. 8ff. [125] Isa. 29. 13.
[126] Mark 10. 18f.

protested that formal observances could not make religion pleasing to God.[127] And Hosea complained that the people of God were destroyed for lack of the right knowledge of God,[128] while Micah clearly expounded the higher values in life, compared with which rivers of oil and thousands of rams were as nothing.[129]

Assignments for Class Reports

1. Who were the contemporary religious leaders? Give a short account of the Pharisees.
2. Why should religious leaders at Jerusalem go to hear a Galilæan layman?
3. Find and report upon the Jewish rules for Sabbath observance in Jesus' time.
4. What justification is there for the name "the ethical prophets," applied to Amos, Hosea, Micah, Isaiah?
5. Can you point out any tradition or institution, especially in the religion of to-day, which could to advantage be restated or reformed, as Jesus restated the marriage law or the nature of the Sabbath?
6. To what extent does Mark thus far lead the reader to believe that he considers Jesus a member of the Jewish church, seeking to reform it from within? What evidence is there to the contrary?
7. As a result of your study thus far, are you inclined to consider the Kingdom of God as something to be realized in the future, or as an ethical program in which Jesus expected his disciples to engage at once? Give reasons for your answer.

The Apocalypse in Mark 13

With the study of this section, an adequate survey of the various addresses, lengthy and brief, of the Master will be completed. It will remain,

[127] Isa. 1. 10ff. [128] Hos. 4. 6. [129] Mic. 6. 6–8.

then, to summarize the ethical teaching of Mark under the topics, first: The Kingdom of God in Mark, and the Messiah-Teacher who proclaimed its imminence; second, the Ethical Relation between men, Jesus, and the Father, taught by Mark as his chief contribution to the Ethics of Jesus.

The discussion, in fact, could proceed without any reference to the thirteenth chapter, or, more particularly, 13. 5b–37, which forms the "apocalypse" of the Gospel. Its omission, however, might raise questions in the student's mind, since the passage in question forms the longest single discourse of Jesus within the second Gospel.

Mark 13. 1–2 forms a very natural approach to the longer address. A disciple remarks upon the massive and beautiful stones of the Temple and the Master returns answer that the building is destined to be destroyed. This conversation is resumed, 13. 3–5a, when Jesus, with Peter, James, John, and Andrew, is somewhere on the Mount of Olives, east of the Temple and the city, looking over toward the wonderful building. Recalling Jesus' remark, the disciples ask him when the destruction of the Temple will happen, and what signs will portend the event. Thereupon Jesus delivers an uninterrupted portrayal of dire happenings, warning his disciples against deceivers who shall come in his name, finally giving an indefinite answer to their question, "When?" but urging to extreme watchfulness.

The discourse properly divides into the following parts: 5–13, warnings for the disciples; 14–23, portents of the coming events and other warnings against false Christs; 24–27, the advent of the Son of man, coming in clouds. Verses 28–37 form an epilog, corresponding to the introduction, or prolog, 1–4.

Verses 30–32 are somewhat in the tone of 9. 1 and in reality give the answer to the disciples' question of verse 4. The writer of the Gospel must have understood (*a*) that Jesus assured his hearers that at least some of those who heard him speak would live to see the spectacular coming of the Son of man on the clouds,[130] and (*b*) that even Jesus was not able to certify precisely the time when this event was to take place.

The historical fact is that the event did not take place when the evangelist, if not Jesus, supposed it would. Later writings of the New Testament cease to emphasize the spectacular arrival of the Son of man upon the clouds and place stress upon the spiritual union of Jesus with those who follow him in the Reign of God.

The destruction of the Temple did occur in 70 A. D., and the words in 13. 2b may be taken as descriptive of this calamity. The tone of 13. 2, "Are you looking upon these great buildings? There shall not be left here a stone upon a stone, which shall not certainly be cast down" is that of a teacher who is trying to turn the attention of his hearers to more permanent things. By the time of the composition of this Gospel, the church at large, well represented by the church in Rome, for which Mark was writing, recognized that the Temple was not the center of Christianity. But the case was otherwise with the men, all of the Jewish church, who stood that day with Jesus on the Mount of Olives.

In the times of Jesus and of Mark, interest in

[130] Compare 14. 62.

that type of literature represented by Daniel in the Jewish Scriptures, and termed by later generations "apocalyptic literature," was very high. It has been satisfactorily established that apocalypticism flourished best in communities where oppressive conditions prevailed.

It is easily possible that Jesus felt the influence of this type of thought and its literary expression in his time, and the evangelist leaves the reader with a clear impression that in his last address to his intimate friends, he discussed these two events, then future to them, the destruction of the Temple and his own return in the clouds.[131]

The element of moral instruction in the chapter is not very large. Positively expressed, the ethical matter is:

> Consider more permanent things than buildings, which can be utterly destroyed.[132] For men will try to lead you astray in my name, after I am gone,[133] and you will be subjected to inquisition, when the danger of personal default will be a real peril.[134] For it is only he who endures to the end who shall find the chief values in life. Be watchful, against dangers within and without,[135] and learn to estimate the real values.

[131] It is not in place to enter upon a critical discussion of this chapter, with its parallels. The student will have become familiar with the various theories concerning it in the study of the Gospels from the point of view of New Testament Introduction. The works of Doctor Charles deal most skillfully with the apocalyptic literature, and the discussions of the term, "Son of man," are legion. This chapter is written in view of the assumption, made at the beginning, that each Gospel represents a unitary work, upon which at least the last editor has put his stamp of approval. The particular task here is to analyze the ethics of each Gospel.

[132] 13. 2. [133] 13. 5, 21f. [134] 13. 9–13. [135] 13. 23, 33–37.

Assignments for Class Reports

1. In what particulars, if any, does chapter 13 modify the conception of the Reign of God as found elsewhere in the Gospel?
2. In what part of the Book of Enoch is found a passage which reminds one of 13. 26 in Mark?
3. Verify the statement that the name "Son of man" is Jesus' own self-designation, with reference to the Gospels only.
4. To what extent does Christianity nowadays take interest in apocalyptic writings?
5. Find instances of apocalyptic writing in the New Testament, outside the Gospels and the Revelation of John.
6. Prepare a brief historical sketch of the destruction of Jerusalem by Titus in 70 A. D.
7. In how many places are the names, "Peter," "James," and "John" found together? In how many places is the name "Andrew" added, as in 13. 3?
8. Assuming that the book of Daniel was written about 164 B. C., what events in the history of the Jews would probably be reflected in that apocalypse?

The Kingdom of God in the Second Gospel and the Messiah-Teacher as its Sponsor

The term, "Kingdom of God," or more clearly expressed, "the Reign of God," was not an invention of any Gospel writer, nor, indeed, of Jesus himself, however much the evangelists may have modified the content of the phrase. Of the canonical writings, the book of Daniel had the largest influence upon Jewish thinking concerning the coming of a new rule of God that should overcome all kingdoms of the earth.[136] The Pharisaic writings that followed

[136] Daniel 2. 1–45.

Daniel, however, were doubtless responsible for a very materialistic expectation concerning the coming Kingdom of God. All pious Israelites, like Joseph of Arimathæa, were "looking for the Reign of God,"[137] and Jesus used words that led his contemporaries to expect that such a "Reign" would come in power.[138] The Teacher also used words to indicate that in a real sense the Reign of God was near to his hearers.[139] See particularly Driver: Daniel, in the *Cambridge Bible for Schools and Colleges*, pp. lxxxv-xc. Men of Jesus' time could "receive the Kingdom,"[140] or, yielding to some hindrance, such as riches[141] or other besetment,[142] might be shut out of the Kingdom.

The disparity between a kingdom that is near and the coming of a Kingdom in power is perhaps explained in the figure of development, which Jesus introduced into some parables of Mark. Either the development of a grain of wheat gradually into a stalk and ear full of grain,[143] or of a small seed into a great plant,[144] points to stages in development. The Reign of God might indeed prevail in some degree, and men might be invited to come under God's sway in a community of persons seeking to do God's will, and yet the coming of that Reign to a place of dominance over other reigns might well be something to expect.

Still another aspect of the Kingdom of God,

---

[137] Mark 15. 43.

[138] 9. 1, "see the Kingdom of God come with power"; 14. 25, "that day when I drink it new in the Kingdom of God."

[139] 1. 15, "the Kingdom of God is at hand"; 12. 34, "not far from the Kingdom."

[140] 10. 15. [141] 10. 23-25. [142] 9. 47. [143] 4. 28.

[144] 4. 31f.

however, is seen in the teaching[145] that men were incapable of knowing all at once the "mysteries" of the new order. Mark shows very clearly that this was the case with the Twelve. But to those who make the Kingdom their chief object of devotion it is given to know the mysteries, and at length these "chosen" become so proficient and experienced that they can teach others.

A unique passage in gospel literature is found in Mark 11. 10: "Blessed be the coming kingdom of our Father David!" The words are part of the ecstatic exclamation of the "many"[146] who took part in the triumphal entrance of Jesus into Jerusalem. This spontaneous celebration was clearly a Messianic outburst on the part of disciples who had come to believe that Jesus really proclaimed the imminence of the Kingdom, yet who misunderstood its nature. It would be entirely in harmony with the views of this evangelist, who sets so clearly before his readers the failure of the Twelve to understand Jesus, to set down also this very Jewish exclamation of these disciples (and probably others) as they enthusiastically sang the Hosanna and part of Psalm 118 as Jesus entered Jerusalem.[147] The expression is not to be understood as in any way expressing Jesus' view of the Reign of God.

While the above references to the Kingdom constitute all that are found in Mark directly mentioning the new order, it will be shown below that Jesus continues to teach about the Reign of God even when the term is not used. In fact, it is probable

---

[145] 4. 11. [146] 11. 8.
[147] The other evangelists omit this sentence acclaiming the coming kingdom of David.

that the most important contribution of the second Gospel to the understanding of the Reign of God is this evangelist's exposition of the ethical relations that exist between men who constitute the Kingdom and between men and God.

The mention above of the enthusiastic acclamation of the "many" who sang "Hosanna" when Jesus entered Jerusalem, and their very Jewish description of the Kingdom as that of "our father David," reminds the reader that at that very moment Jesus was advancing to an unparalleled discipline of suffering and to death.

These pages have already emphasized the failure of Jesus' contemporaries to understand him, a fact so apparent to Mark that here in his Gospel he has quite fully expounded the Christian view of the Messiah as his own generation and church had come to understand him. He was the Messiah-Teacher, who served, suffered and died, a consistent witness to the spirit of that community whose Herald he was and whose Ruler was the Father.

Jesus, to the Second Evangelist, was a man of tremendous social sympathy, who never refused helpful service to any who needed. From the beginning of his ministry to the end Mark indicates a path for Jesus which was strewn with human wreckage, much of which was salvaged. From being social liabilities, men become social assets; from being dependents upon the community, now restored in limb and faculties, men become workers. The list of healings in the Gospel is impressive. An insane man in the synagogue at Capernaum,[148]

[148] I. 23ff.

Simon's wife's mother,[149] a crowd of persons, ill and demented,[150] a leper,[151] a palsied man,[152] a man with a withered hand,[153] the Gerasene demoniac,[154] Jairus' daughter and the woman with a hemorrhage,[155] the daughter of the Greek woman,[156] the deaf man who could not speak plainly, privately healed,[157] the blind man of Bethsaida,[158] the demented child whom the disciples could not heal,[159] Bartimæus at Jericho's gate,[160] together with instances of numbers together,[161] are catalogued by Mark to show to what an extent Jesus practiced this social ministry. This openness to the appeal for help was not inconsistent with his admonition to service.

To the Twelve the Teacher declared that it was his own lot to suffer and die,[162] and his words seem to the modern reader entirely unambiguous. And in the time of the evangelist this personal feature of the Master's ethical program was recognized as an appropriate element in the program of the Kingdom.

Jesus' interest in and compassion for people was spontaneous.[163] He offered his example as worthy of the disciples' emulation, and, true to his conviction that personal service to men is the best way to bring about a brotherhood among men and to establish a close ethical relation between man and man, and between men and the Father, he went to his death, saying: "The Son of man came . . . to serve, and to give his life a ransom for many."

[149] 1. 30f. [150] 1. 32–34. [151] 1. 40ff.
[152] 2. 3ff. [153] 3. 1ff. [154] 5. 2ff. [155] 5. 22–43.
[156] 7. 25ff. [157] 7. 32ff. [158] 8. 22ff. [159] 9. 14ff.
[160] 10. 46ff. [161] 1. 39; 3. 10; 6. 5, 55.
[162] 8. 31; 9. 9f., 31; 10. 33; 14. 8, 18–21, 27, 41.
[163] 6. 34; 8. 2; 10. 21; 14. 38.

The Messiah of Mark is a teacher of men, a servant of all, the Servant of God.

Assignments for Class Reports

1. What passages in Isaiah are called "the servant passages"?
2. What traits of the "servant of Jehovah" has Mark appropriated for use in his delineation of Jesus? Are these in the nature of direct quotation or otherwise?
3. Why is the term "Kingdom" less appropriate to-day than it was in the first century as a designation of the movement inaugurated by Jesus? What term could be used to-day?
4. What "Pharisaic writings" contained references to the Kingdom of God?
5. What religions in the Roman Empire of the first century taught in so-called "mysteries"?
6. After a study of the four narratives of the triumphal entrance of Jesus into Jerusalem, what conclusion do you reach as to the personnel of the "many" who sang "Hosanna"? How widely known did this event become immediately? What was Jesus' attitude toward the proceedings?
7. What elements of organization, if any, are ascribed by Mark to the Kingdom of God?

Ethical Values Within the New Brotherhood

From the foregoing exposition of the Reign of God the person and conduct of Jesus are seen to be illustrative of his conception of the new order, according to the second Gospel. In this section, devoted to a final summary of the ethical teaching of Mark's Gospel, the relations between all persons concerned in the Reign of God are to be traced.

In his presentation of the important teaching which has been analyzed Mark had before him some cardinal principle of the moral life to which other subjects, namely, the Messiahship of Jesus, the identity of the Son of man and his future coming on the clouds of heaven, the public ministry of Jesus, the mission of the Twelve, and even the Passion story, were all subordinated. This principle was something that concerned men's daily intercourse in all social and business relations and human life in all its phases, including the fellowship of men with the Father of all. This was no other than the principle of living together, the establishment of ethical relations between men.

The best point of departure for the exposition of this principle is doubtless found in that incident near the end of Jesus' life when the disciples discussed acrimoniously their individual chances of preferment.[164] Two of their number tried to obtain the coveted preferment by direct appeal. The answer of Jesus was that greatness or prominence among those who live the life of the Kingdom is not an assigned favor.[165] No outward mark or office makes a man ethically superior. This "greatness," however, can be won. It is an achievement wrought by unselfish service of others and is illustrated not only in the words of Jesus but in his example, "for the Son of man came not to be served, but to serve."

A second important saying, which is fully as fundamental to Mark's exposition of ethical relations between men and Jesus and, through him, between men and the Father, is 3. 33–35:

---

[164] 9. 34; 10. 35.

[165] 9. 35b–37; 10. 42b–45.

"He said, Who is my mother and my brothers? and after surveying those seated about him in a circle, he said: Behold my mother and my brothers; whosoever does the will of God, the same is my brother and sister and mother."

With these sayings in chapters 3, 9 and 10 in mind, as the key to Jesus' teaching in Mark as to the heart of the moral life, further insight into the method of the evangelist will show that the authority of Jesus, the joyous fellowship between Master and disciples, and the practical ethics of the community which they formed, all become of service in exhibiting the "mystery of the Kingdom" as the Christians of the seventh decade of the first century understood it.

Back of the call of the first disciples there was an evident authority. This was clear even to the many who heard the Master publicly,[166] and it became apparent to religious leaders, who explained it in their own fashion.[167] Mark thinks of the great Teacher as a commanding personality. Even powers in the mysterious spirit world recognized his authority,[168] and the cosmic forces obeyed his behest.[169] But as shown by the preponderance of private teaching in this Gospel,[170] it was to the disciples that this authority appeared most clearly and most powerfully.[171]

The fellowship between Jesus and the disciples appeared to Mark to be, for the period of their instruction, somewhat joyous. The disciples, said Jesus, do not fast while he is with them,[172] notwithstanding much of their time is spent among

---

[166] 1. 22, 27b; 2. 10. [167] 3. 22b.
[168] 1. 27b, 34b; 3. 11f.; 5. 7. [169] 4. 39–41. [170] Pages 21ff.
[171] See 8. 29. [172] 2. 18–20.

the outcast and miserable,[173] the very numerous folk whose plight might well excite pity and lead to pessimism. But the Teacher does not take a somber view of life to the "sinners" and the sick, who have need of a cheerful physician.

This group of men under the tutelage of Jesus were brought into contact, not only with the poor, the outcast, the sick, but with the mentally deranged, thus invading that which seemed to the man of that time a supernatural realm, where demons lurked, ready to possess the body of an unfortunate,[174] and where the men so "possessed" were vividly referred to as the spirits themselves.[175] Here magic formulas could bind one's tongue,[176] but the authority that was in Jesus could unloose the "bond of the tongue," open the blind eyes or make the deaf to hear, despite demonic influence. It was in this realm that the power of effective prayer on Jesus' part exorcised a demon who resisted the delegated authority of the disciples.[177]

A note of optimism, although not an empty and enthusiastic optimism, and which frequently becomes infectious, always dominates the words of the Teacher.[178]

To our evangelist, this fellowship, glad, optimistic, constructive, had as its function the establishment of a real devotion to the Master, in a bond not only of service but of likeness. Even when Peter failed to understand clearly what sort of Messiah Jesus was, his avowal of loyalty[179] and

[173] 2. 15–17. [174] 5. 1–4.
[175] 3. 11f.; 8. 33b. [176] 7. 35b.
[177] 7. 37; 9. 29; compare 6. 7.
[178] 4. 29, "harvest is come," 5. 36, "fear not, only believe."
[179] 14. 29.

adventure into personal danger,[180] despite his denial, revealed his fundamental allegiance to his Master in his own person. The literature of the apostolic age is unanimous in ascribing to this apostle a primacy which was not so much due to ecclesiastical appointment as to personal achievement.

The practical ethics of the small community made up of Jesus and his disciples (probably many more than twelve), finds exposition in a number of places. One of the late lessons[181] was one of the most practical and fundamental. This was the lesson of dependence upon God, the word being "faith." The shriveled fig tree was an object lesson, which Mark brings out in the staccato, "Have faith in God," when the disciple spoke his wonder. If one depend upon the Father, what power is in one's band! This tree is as nothing. When the little hand in the tossing boat was terrified[182] the Master asked, "Why are you afraid? Have you no faith?" This quality in a man was fundamental to entrance into the Kingdom. Of course it was necessary as an element of Kingdom-living.

The brotherhood involved in the existence of ethical relations between members of the community was based upon the older moral codes. "Whenever you stand in prayer, forgive, if you have anything against anyone."[183] The ancient moral maxim of the Shema[184] is a basis for Kingdom life.[185] In few words, for Jesus' ethics in all the Gospels seem reducible to but few principles, the man of the

---

[180] 14. 47, 54. [181] 11. 22.
[182] 4. 40. [183] 11. 25. [184] Deut. 6. 4f.
[185] Mark 12. 29ff.

Kingdom regards his fellowman unselfishly rather than with a view to his exploitation. And selfishness of all forms is alien to the men who live under the Reign of God.

Assignments for Class Reports

1. In what way is the authority of Jesus exhibited in the call of his early disciples? References, 1. 17, 20; 2. 14; 6. 7ff.
2. Explain in modern terms the remark of the evangelist that the disciples' "heart was hardened," 6. 52.
3. What evidence for or against the thesis that Jesus believed in the reality of demons is found in this Gospel?
4. What is probably the modern explanation of the phenomena which early Christian writers termed demon possession?
5. What personal ethical values do you find in Mark 8. 34–36, expressed in terms most familiar to members of the class?
6. What practical result would follow if an entire community, for example, a college community, adopted the program which Mark teaches as the program of the Kingdom?

CHAPTER III

THE ETHICS OF THE GOSPEL ACCORDING TO MATTHEW

Analysis of the Discourse Element in Matthew

The Gospel according to Matthew is the ethical Gospel *par excellence.* The work is written from the standpoint of the conservative side of early Christianity, emphasizing the fulfillment of the Jewish Scriptures in the life and teaching of Jesus. In the spirit of many of the Jewish books, this evangelist often puts into his portrayal of Jesus' work passages that show his reader how sympathetic the Master was with the prevailing moral teaching.[1]

Compared with Mark, with its 11,271 words, 4,006 of which were words of Jesus, the first Gospel contains 18,499 words, of which 10,489 are words spoken by the Master.[2] The narrative material of Mark comprises a total of 7,267 words, as compared with 7,880 of Matthew. The difference in length between Mark and Matthew is thus seen to be almost entirely in discourse or teaching material. The narrative of Matthew is, according to authorities upon the synoptic Gospels, almost entirely taken

[1] See 5. 17; 8. 4; 9. 13; 12. 7; 15. 7–9; 19. 17–19; and other passages.

[2] The count is on the basis of Westcott and Hort's Greek text.

over from Mark by the First Evangelist,[3] although it is to be noted that each evangelist lets his own style predominate.

The structure of the first Gospel, then, presents the appearance of a narrative framework within which are placed with fine literary skill words and discourses which well indicate to the reader the interest of the evangelist in ethical teaching.

Jesus in the first Gospel is the Teacher throughout. In training his disciples he expends fine exegesis upon the Torah, approves all the weightier matters of the moral law, quotes the ethical prophets with glowing approval, and declares the imminence of a moral order which will preserve all the best in the old yet which will bring out moral truth in social application as never before understood. Here Jesus is no heavenly dreamer. His interest is decidedly in the life that men are living in this world. The Kingdom of God will harmonize to some extent with their dreams of a new economic order, for it will be bound up with the daily life of men, but, contrary to their dreams, its approach will be other than militant.

Matthew has a frequently noted tendency to collect teaching material into long discourses. Of these, chapters 5, 6, 7 contain the Sermon on the Mount (1,937 words), chapter 10, the address to the Twelve (639 words), chapter 18 (613 words, inter-

[3] William Sanday, in *Oxford Studies in the Synoptic Problem*, p. 3. estimates that of the six hundred and sixty-one verses of Mark, "all but some fifty verses have been actually incorporated in the other two Gospels," and H. B. Swete, in his *Commentary on St. Mark*, p. lxix, points out that of the one hundred and six sections of Mark, but three are wholly absent from Matthew and Luke together, and of the remainder ninety-six sections are to be found in Matthew.

rupted once by a question from Peter), chapter 23 (638 words), chapter 24 (745 words in uninterrupted discourse, plus 17 in verse 2), chapter 25 (751 words). Thus a total of 5,323 words (Greek) are placed by Matthew in six solid blocks of discourse.

But there are other collections of Jesus' words which, although interrupted more or less by interjections or questions, form important discourses in this Gospel. Chapter 11 (406 words in four groups), chapter 12 (602 words in six groups), chapter 13 (843 words in eight groups, but slightly divided by narrative), chapters 19–20 (687 words in seventeen groups, the largest, 308 words, extending from 19. 28 to 20. 16), chapter 21 (425 words in ten groups), and chapter 22 (397 words in eight groups).

Conversational connectives are most numerous in chapters 4, 8, 9, 16, 17, and 26. The last mentioned chapter corresponds to Mark 14, in which, as noted above, there is found a large amount of dialog.

Some of the discourse material is to be found in both Mark and Matthew, notably the parable of the Soils,[4] the discussion of the purpose of parables, following this parable, together with the explanation of the parable privately to the disciples, the parable of the Mustard Seed (Small Beginnings), the discussion of ceremonial and real uncleanness,[5] the definition of "the greatest,"[6] and the discussion of such social questions as divorce and wealth,[7] together with a number of smaller and perhaps less important passages.

---

[4] Mark 4. 1–9; Matt. 13. 1–9.
[5] Mark 7. 1–23; Matt. 15. 1–20.
[6] Mark 9. 33–37; Matt. 18. 1–5.
[7] Mark 10. 1–12, 17–31; Matt. 19. 1–12, 16–30.

ACCORDING TO MATTHEW

In summarizing the distribution of the teaching material in the first Gospel it is noted that the writer has a tendency to group the words of Jesus into longer discourses, that he uses most of the discourse material as well as the narrative material of Mark, but adds considerably to the former. The most conspicuous of the ethical discourses are the Sermon on the Mount,[8] the Address to the Twelve, as they go out upon their mission,[9] Discussions of Institutional and Ceremonial Matters with the Religious Leaders,[10] The Parables of the Kingdom,[11] Exposition of the Law of Mutual Relationships,[12] Social Principles within the Kingdom,[13] Parable of Gracious Justice,[14] and the Discourses of Passion Week.[15]

Assignments for Class Reports

1. Report upon three instances of Jesus' approval of the Jewish moral law. Is his approval unqualified?
2. How many instances of approving quotation from the prophets can you find on Jesus' lips in this Gospel? Give references.
3. Compare Matthew with Mark in the use of parables.
4. In what respects, if any, do Jesus' discourses resemble the formal lectures of a teacher of ethics?
5. What differences, if any, appear between Mark and Matthew in the use of questions on Jesus' lips? Does Jesus in both Gospels alike ask questions with a view to gaining information?
6. Find the most descriptive names for the parables spoken during Passion Week, according to Matthew.
7. Point out as many quotations as possible from the prophets made by the evangelist.

---

[8] Chapters 5–6–7. [9] Chapter 10. [10] Chapters 12 and 15.
[11] Chapter 13. [12] Chapter 18. [13] Chapter 19.
[14] Chapter 20. [15] Chapters 21–25 inclusive.

8. What are the regular formulas used by this evangelist to introduce parables? Point out any parbles not introduced by such a formula.
9. If you were to select five discourses in this Gospel containing its most intensely ethical material, which chapters or parts of chapters would you name? What titles would best fit these five discourses?
10. Estimate the relative proportion of Old Testament words used by Jesus (a) in chapter 13; (b) in chapter 19; (c) in chapter 23.

Outline of the Sermon on the Mount

The study of Matthæan ethics begins properly with the largest and most comprehensive discourse within the first Gospel, which is quite universally termed the Sermon on the Mount. Considered in its form as found in Chapters 5, 6, and 7, this moral document constitutes a most engaging survey of the chief themes upon which Jesus delivered himself. No portion of any Gospel surpasses these three chapters in importance for the student of the ethics of the Gospels.

For the purpose of clearness, an outline and synopsis of the Sermon on the Mount will be offered at this point.

Introduction: Matt. 5. 1–16.

A composite portrait of a potential member of that community which is both defined as and characterized by the Reign of God.

The several beatitudes indicate varied aspects of character and outward conditions experienced by members of the new brotherhood, while the

Salt and Light metaphors point out the function of those who qualify.[16]

I. *The Moral Order as Taught by Jesus, and its Relation to the Current Jewish Ethics.* 5. 17–48.

1. The Law survives as an integral part of the new order,[17] such a social order as the most optimistic of the prophets had hoped for. But in this Reign of God, the "rightness" of the men who constitute the ethical community from now on must be better, finer, more exacting than that type of character demanded by the teaching of contemporary professional teachers in the synagogues.
2. What, then, is this "more exacting" or "exceeding" right-ness? It is illustrated thus.[18]
   a. Murder, so far from being alone judged as an evil deed, is seen to be instigated by even hateful thought. Thus, under the Reign of God no grudge should be allowed to lodge and grow. From small differences come serious consequences.[19]
   b. Adultery, a product of unsocial and impure thinking, leads to social disintegration, to disruption of the family and to the degradation of the individual.[20]
   (*i*) Since unsocial passions arise from unsocial thinking and evil imagination, the reconstruction of the thought-life is demanded even if radical measures are needed. Only a pure mind can guarantee moral conduct.[21]

[16] 5. 3–16. [17] 5. 17–20. [18] 5. 21–48. [19] 5. 21–26.
[20] 5. 27–32. [21] 5. 27–30.

(*ii*) Divorce, as a menace to an ethically sound monogamy, finds its strength in the weakness of a superficial morality. In the Reign of God, the marriage relation in its ideal form is guaranteed by pure motives, emotions, and thoughts.[22]

c. The taking of oaths, as practised according to ancient precepts and contemporary teaching, leads to casuistry and actual reversal of the avowed purpose of such vows. Often moral values are voided by the clever use of pious formulas. In a strictly ethical regime, personal integrity is such that oaths are not needed. "Yea" in word is but the expression of a "Yea" of the inner life.[23]

d. Retaliation is currently justified upon the basis of certain ancient words. But men are by nature so constituted that the sway of such a law and practice arouses dormant selfishness and revengeful motives that are not easily satisfied. This makes for social disintegration. But the Reign of God makes for social integration. Thus, instead of the rule of eye for eye, life for life, the surpassing standard of living demanded within the new moral order adopts the constructive attitude. This, so far from demanding revenge, insists upon no right for its own sake, but cooperates in building up ami-

[22] 5. 31–32. [23] 5. 33–37.

cable relationships and developing a real brotherhood.[24]

e. In the spirit of the preceding rule, a high test of the "surpassing righteousness" of any member of the ethical brotherhood is found in his ability to love the unlovely. For this is what the Father does. Men thus "become sons of the Father," as they acquire the will to be generous toward the unlovely and unkind.[25]

II. *The Reign of God in its Social Evidences.* Matt. 6. 1–34.

1. There are ethical values in religious functions, beyond their form. These values are reflected in the community life most favorably when the religious form is properly evaluated by the individual who makes use of it. Illustrations in particular are philanthropy, prayer, and fasting.[26]

a. In philanthropy, ethical values reside not so much in the formal performance of a duty as in unostentatious and sympathetic help. Ostentation and publicity in themselves reflect self-interest. The moral community is enriched by unselfish and sympathetic men.[27]

b. Prayer may be but a form, but a "son of the Father" knows his own ethical relationship and best attains fellowship with the Father in private prayer. Only when prayer becomes a personal relation does

[24] 5. 38–42. [25] 5. 43–48. [26] 6. 1–18. [27] 6. 1–4.

its ethical force react upon the community.[28] Not by mere phrases can one enter into fellowship with God,[29] yet if an illustration be asked for, it is found in the model prayer.[30]

c. Fasting is not an exercise devised to exhibit one's virtue or piety to others. When effective it is essentially a personal affair between the "son".and the Father.[31]

2. Personal values in the moral community take precedence over all other alleged worth.[32]

a. One who depends upon material wealth thereby evidences a bent unworthy of the Reign of God. "For where thy treasure is, there thy heart is as well." Personal values are not subject to damage by moth or rust, nor can thieves take them away. Highest values are apart from the material things so often eagerly sought.[33]

b. Generosity marks the "son of the Father." The "son" will use wealth, but will not abuse it. The difference lies in the end toward which it is used. The "single eye" signifies the opposite of niggardliness and selfishness.[34]

c. Loyalty is normal within the truly ethical community. It is impossible to divide allegiance between competing interests. Unity of attitude, entirety of devotion to personal interests, and unselfishness in

---

[28] 6. 5–15. [29] 6. 7. [30] 6. 9–15. [31] 6. 16–18.
[32] 6. 19–34. [33] 6. 19–21. [34] 6. 22–23.

the use of all advantage characterize the citizen of such a community.[35]

d. If (a) one is not to emphasize wealth, if (b) one is to be generous with one's possessions, and if (c) one cannot find any mean between emphasis upon personal and material values, the question arises, "How then, shall *my* needs be met?" The personal, solicitous interest of the Father in his children furnishes the answer. Not one's needs, but one's character, in fact, the possession of the Father's nature through sonship,[36] is to be first considered. Supreme trust in the provident will of the Father is the rule.[37]

III. *The Rule of Reciprocity Within the Ethical Community, and Other Practical Tests of its Citizens.* 7. 1–23.

1. In the Reign of God all tests of character or determination of values in the community life proceed under certain laws. There is a reciprocity that is commendable, for it is constructive. But arbitrary and partial critical judgments lead to a reciprocal judgment and an attitude which bars progress.[38] Self-examination is more rational than judgment of others, and must precede any attempt to evaluate others' deeds. Yet values must be discerned and in the course of life moral judgments must be made.[39]

---

[35] 6. 24. [36] 5. 43ff. [37] 6. 25–34. [38] 7. 1–2.
[39] Matt. 7. 1–6. See 10. 15; 7. 6, 15f.

2. Not hasty judgment, but cooperation, characterizes the worthy man. Reciprocity of the constructive sort is practiced in the daily life of the Kingdom. The Father furnishes an example, for the earnest seeker will find; to him that asks, the needed boon will be given,[40] and such a regime begets in the kingdom-minded the supreme type of reciprocity, whereby each one vies with every other in measuring service to his fellow by his own need and desire.[41]
3. Admission to that ethical community in which the sway of God and his right-ness is supreme is open to the discerning. But kingdom-values will not be obvious to those whose interests are selfish. The figure of a narrow door illustrates the ease with which self-absorption excludes from the better life those under a program of self-seeking. The broad way is easy to follow.[42]
4. "By their fruits you shall know them," twice stated (7. 16, 20), constitutes a pronouncement of the normative power of the inner or real nature. Here is judgment, to be sure. The prophet who takes but the form of a prophet, the user of phrases which have no content, the tree or vine that is unfruitful, illustrate the principle that a valid moral life depends upon the directive force and informing nature of the attitude or motive. Even if men fail to discern the false, still the Father, whose nature true sons possess, will declare, "I never knew you."[43]

[40] Matt. 7. 7–11. [41] 7. 12. [42] 7. 13–14. [43] 7. 15–23.

CONCLUSION: Matt. 7. 24–27.

The foregoing principles are so inextricably associated with the life that men live that it may be said solemnly of all who take them otherwise than seriously and with acceptance, that they are like men who deliberately or ignorantly build upon an insecure foundation. The tests of life make such a man at length ridiculous. But the serious and practical hearer and user of these sound principles will build his character as a superstructure upon an enduring basis. His character endures because from within outward, and from below upward it is sound.

ASSIGNMENTS FOR CLASS REPORTS

1. After study of the foregoing summary analysis, devise the best subject to place above the Sermon on the Mount.
2. What verse or verses best express the theme that dominates the whole of the Sermon?
3. How much of the Sermon can be found in Mark?
4. Since a certain similarity between the narratives of Mark and Matthew has been indicated, find the place in Mark's narrative where this Sermon could properly be inserted.
5. How does the Sermon on the Plain in Luke compare quantitatively with the Sermon on the Mount?
6. Discuss the statement that the Sermon is in substance "primitive preaching of Christianity." See Burkitt, *Gospel History and Its Transmission*, p. 39.
7. Is it probable that 5. 13–16 applies to the apostles only? Who were the hearers of the Sermon, according to Matthew's context?
8. Does the analysis indicate that, in the estimation of the evangelist, Jesus broke away from Judaism, or that he built upon Judaism?

9. On psychological grounds, how does the Sermon thus far appeal to you as an example of instruction addressed to unlearned men and women?
10. To what extent should one distinguish between the present literary form of the Sermon on the Mount and Jesus' oral address to the disciples?

The Sermon on the Mount: Character and Function of Those Who Qualify for the New Order

The interpretation of the Sermon on the Mount properly starts out from its setting—geographical, historical, and literary. Involved are also economic conditions of its time, religious practice and hopes. The Sermon itself is in literary form which it took more than a generation after the words which it reports were spoken; so, in fact, if there be such a difference, the interpreter must think first of these circumstances as they influence first its literary form, and then of those conditions which attended the spoken words. It seems highly probable that the attendant conditions would not be the same in both instances.

The evangelist understands that most of the hearers were poor,[44] that many were lame, blind, deaf, dumb, or crippled in various ways,[45] some were of unsound mind, (possessed with demons), and all doubtless were oppressed by excessive tax-levies, to which the publicans added what they could,[46]

[44] 11. 5b.
[45] 11. 4f.; 4. 23–25; 9. 2, 27ff., 32.
[46] Matt. 9. 36. The translation of this passage in most versions is too complimentary to the Jewish authorities. The people were subject to exploitation, compare Mark 12. 40. They were victims of social injustice and hence were heartily discouraged and without adequate religious leadership.

and the common people were despised generally by the upper classes.

It is to be assumed that any address made by Jesus would first of all have his immediate hearers in mind. And it is as necessary to assume that any address of Jesus in its literary form a generation or more later would have both hearers and readers in mind. It is fair to suppose, then, that in its present literary form the Sermon on the Mount is likely to perpetuate much of the original form of expression, at least in so far as the express statements of the context demand.

The opening of the discourse alludes to conditions recently viewed by Jesus,[47] and presented in the multitude of 5.1, who had come from far and wide,[48] thus the mention of the "poor," "they who mourn," the hungry and thirsty, and the "persecuted."

Certain it is that the physical aspects of hunger, mourning, oppression, care, even "anxious care" for the daily bread, characterized Jesus' audience, not only on one occasion, but many.

It might well appear ironical to speak to such people of the coming "Reign of God," yet it is directly affirmed of the "poor in spirit" and of the "persecuted" that "theirs is the Kingdom of heaven."[49]

"How is it possible to think of a Reign of God under such circumstances as these?" must have been the substance of questioning among many

---

[47] Matt. 4. 24.

[48] 4. 25 says, "from Galilee, Decapolis, Jerusalem and Judæa; and from beyond Jordan."

[49] 5. 3, 10.

who heard Jesus speak those words of promise.[50]

The answer of Jesus to such questioning is found in the pericope usually called the Beatitudes, which is correctly described as a composite portrait of one who, in spite of circumstances that appear in themselves to militate against such a Reign of Righteousness, is eligible to its happiness. Just as an introduction to a well-wrought address gives in a comprehensive way the thought of the whole, so the Beatitudes and the sayings about "salt" and "light" assure the readers that the highest type of ethical progress and its satisfaction ("happy"), may be compatible with human circumstances.

To paraphrase this pericope:[51]

> The Reign of God is a practicable moral program for such men as these peasants upon the hillside, many of whom have a very restricted mental horizon. It may be said, vividly, that the happiness of such a social order is theirs, as it is, indeed, for all, even the afflicted, whose sorrow marks their faces, yet which cannot obstruct the inevitable comfort. Even a man who is by nature no user of force, one of a class who scarcely dare to claim any right as theirs, is happy indeed, for within the new order the promise of a rich inheritance will be made good, as no forcible taking or insistent demanding could bring it about.[52] There are, indeed, the hungry and thirsty now, who do not receive at once the water and

[50] The term "kingdom of God" is practically synonymous with that used chiefly by Matthew, "kingdom of heaven." Compare the expressions, "God bless you!" and "Heaven bless you!"

[51] 5. 3–16.

[52] "Inherit the earth"; see Deut. 4. 22 and Lev. 20. 24.

the loaf, but no longing for right and good will be denied. Men may be under the very sway of God and still experience untoward things, but the fuller coming of the Reign of God will correct even the outward, economic ills. A man who knows best the meaning of that "Happy" of the Old Testament beatitude will in the new era be a man of merciful turn of mind, right in his attitudes, pure in his thoughts, seeking peaceable relations between himself and others and among his brothers. Such a character will warrant the very expectation of seeing God, for such men are the very "sons of the Father!"

Men of such character, like salt, are a synonym for wholesomeness and life. Their lives stand for all that is vital and vitalizing. Like light, the men of the kingdom shed a radiance upon the way of others. That way which their lives illuminate leads to the upper levels of life. The light of their worthy deeds attracts men, not to themselves, but to God, under whose sway they live.

In this introduction to the Sermon the First Evangelist has without doubt made use of genuine teaching of Jesus, even though he has adopted a literary form and outline which is original with the writer. A comparison of the Third Gospel, with any harmony of the Gospels in hand, will assure the student of this. The evangelist thinks of the immediate disciples of Jesus as the auditors, at least at the beginning, for Jesus goes into the mountain to avoid the multitude.[53] At the close of the

[53] 5. 1.

discourse, however, the "multitudes"[54] were present, leaving the reader to visualize the gradual assembling of the many who could reach the retreat of Jesus and his disciples, and others would be visible to the hearers who themselves could not hear.

Whatever the exact historical situation, the evangelist, in his literary expression of Jesus' fundamental moral precepts, makes it very plain that human conditions as they were found in Jesus' time were not considered by the Master as cause for exclusion from the sway of a new morally sound social order which he was inaugurating. On the contrary, these untoward conditions were acting as the incentive to bring in the new order as quickly as possible.

In summary upon the Introduction to the Sermon, it should be pointed out that in Jesus' mind, as the evangelist understood him, the field of moral endeavor is the world of men as it is. All are called but all do not qualify. Jesus has begun the instruction of certain men whom he particularly addresses under the metaphors of "salt" and "light." He promises here no riches, not even absence of physical want; he promises no high position in government, no degree of authority over their weaker fellows, nor does he propose national preeminence for Israel. The advantages that connote the "happiness" that shall be theirs are couched in what are usually termed "spiritual terms." But the terms of the evangelist do not thereby connote remote fulfillment or supernatural staging of a happy existence. As far as one can see, Matthew

---

[54] 7. 28.

reports words of Jesus that assure the evangelist's contemporaries of the possible Reign of God within and among them, a reign not so much outwardly organized as it would be outwardly and inwardly salutary.

Many of the hints in this introduction[55] find exposition in the following portions of the Sermon.

Assignments for Class Reports

1. Find and report upon as many causes as possible of the distressing economic conditions of Jesus' time.
2. To what extent and in what way is sanitation a moral measure?
3. Find as many instances as possible of beatitudes in the Old Testament.
4. Does "Blessed" ("Happy") in the beatitudes signify that Jesus taught that happiness was an end in itself? Define "beatitude."

The Sermon on the Mount: Right-ness That Surpasses That of the Contemporary Synagogue Teaching

Jesus was not an accredited rabbi. Not long after he began his public ministry, there is reason to believe, he was refused the use of Jewish synagogues to teach. This compelled outdoor activity. In any event, Jesus would have been compelled to teach out of doors because of the larger number that attended his ministry.

The Sermon on the Mount represents such outdoor instruction, and it is probably no accident that the First Evangelist places at the beginning of the discourse Jesus' defense against the charge

[55] Matt. 5. 3–16.

that had been made (implicit in 5.17), that his teaching was destructive. From the evangelist's point of view, the Sermon is apologetic to a certain degree. To paraphrase Matthew, 5. 17–20:

> You are far from right in supposing that I teach contrary to the law or the prophets. On the contrary, I love these scriptures and I would have them utterly fulfilled. I am myself fulfilling them, in the sense that I am seeking to make their real meaning plain.
>
> In the Kingdom of heaven it is the man who brings forth the truest meaning of these ancient writings, and teaches this meaning to his fellows who is really a worthy man. But how many try to belittle or misteach what the prophets taught so plainly! If in any particular teaching I seem to depart from the teaching of the synagogues, look into the writings themselves and see whether the scribes themselves have not erred. Of a truth, I declare to you men of the present that you must possess and express a character, a morality, that surpasses that of these professional teachers, if you are to be worthy to be included in the Reign of God.

This statement on the part of Jesus might well provoke the question which is implicit between verses 20 and 21: "What do you mean by a morality that surpasses that of our professional teachers? Are they not our scribes?[56] or, again, Can you not explain further what you mean by "righteousness

[56] The term "scribe" meant to Jesus' contemporaries, "teacher of religion," or "a man instructed in traditional truth," hence the force of their remark that Jesus did not teach "like the scribes."

that shall exceed that of the scribes and Pharisees"? Verses 21–48 of chapter 5 contain *in extenso* the further exposition of this "exceeding righteousness," with illustrations from the law and other parts of the Scriptures.

In the expressions, "Ye have heard,—" and "It was said,"[57] are recognized conventional formulas which introduce a quotation from Scripture. In each one of these places where Scripture is quoted, one finds Jesus' own statement of the truth in the matter. He asserts an authority at least equal to that of the Scripture in question, and in the understanding of the evangelist, no scribe could claim greater insight than Jesus exhibited.

But this in no way urges to the conclusion that in every case Jesus set his own view over against that of the law and prophets. As in the case of oaths,[58] Jesus may, indeed, set the scriptural statement aside, but again, as in the case of two quotations from the Decalog,[59] the Master offers an exegesis of the words which, so far from opposing the commandment, brings out its real meaning, which contemporary instruction had overlooked.

Withal, the evangelist is extremely in sympathy with the view expressed by Jesus' hearers, and no doubt it was heartily believed in Matthew's time that Jesus "taught with authority, and not as the scribes."[60]

This exposition of the "exceeding righteousness," in brief paraphrase, reads:[61]

> There is an old commandment, with penalty, that reads: Do not kill. Yet I assure you that

[57] 5. 21, 27, 31, 33, 38, 43. [58] 5. 33–37. [59] 5. 21ff., 27ff.
[60] 7. 29. [61] Matt. 5. 21–48.

the same penalty is valid for the angry attitude, yea for the hateful or contemptuous epithet. Do not suppose that you can worship with acceptance when quarrels or dissensions exist between you and your fellow man. The "exceeding righteousness" of which I spoke involves recognition of this great truth, and a practice in harmony with it.

Another commandment says: Do not commit adultery. But the scripture also forbids all that leads to adultery. The lustful gaze is not without its guilt. It is worth the most drastic measures to keep the fountain clear. The body is less than the life. The old law about divorce had not so much truth in it as the scribes suppose. Beware of making a wife an adulteress, or involving another man in sin, by easily divorcing a woman, unless, indeed, it be on serious moral grounds.

Consider the old word about oath-taking! It is better to cancel than to observe this saying as is customary. The demands of the "exceeding right-ness" are such that one is not obliged to recommend his honesty by an appeal to Deity. The moral character of a man of the Kingdom is such that his straightforward statement suffices. Do not use oaths: express yourself simply.

There is one ancient saying which has in it such a wrong principle that it must be replaced in the new order. This is the law of retaliation, an eye for an eye, a life for a life. This rule serves to bring out the vicious and must be superseded by a positive law of nonresistance. Do not insist upon your rights for selfish reasons. Better be defrauded, better go twice the legal distance, than give place to destructive motives. The "exceeding right-ness" of the new order cannot be developed under any regime of revenge.

Last and most important of all, the surpassing character is so patterned after the known generosity and kindliness of the heavenly Father that the possessor of this "exceeding" worth may be called a "son of the Father." But this involves the use of standards not usually praised, nor popularly espoused. Love the unlovely; pray for your persecutors; not waiting to see whether they love you first, or greet you first. This is the essence of the Father's attitude toward men. Such is the surpassing righteousness of the Kingdom.

The command, "Thou shalt not kill," is quoted with entire approval. But within the new ethical community all that contributes to a murderous act will be closely guarded. At no place in the Sermon is it more plainly stated than here that in the thought of Jesus, as the evangelist sets it forth, all behavior is conditioned by the set of the mind. Certain emotional attitudes, deliberate plotting, cherishing tabooed emotions all determine the set of the mind.

No brotherhood can safely exist upon merely formal precepts. The brotherhood of the Kingdom is based upon a spiritual discipline.

Jesus' exposition of the higher righteousness emphasizes the right of the family to exist as a worthy Kingdom institution. The morality of the community is, in fact, conserved by the preservation of the family's purity. Jesus' illustration taken from family ethics makes plain his view that the Kingdom of the heavens, in Matthew's phrase, in actually at home upon earth. For this same evangelist quotes Jesus to the effect that in the after life no marriage is known.[62]

Thus, in the moral program of men and women among whom the sway of God prevails, even "mental adultery" will be inhibited. For by the very constitution of the Kingdom, there cannot exist unchallenged any clearly defined inclination to an unfilial or unsocial act. The evangelist, however, does not assume that all who are actually within the Kingdom maintain rigidly at all times this strict discipline. Unhappily, there may happen even such impurity in act as to warrant the divorce of the untrue member, possibly in the interest of the group.[63]

In the pericope, 5. 33-37, the First Evangelist teaches that the oath, as currently practiced, was in fact immoral. "Swear not at all," said Jesus. To utter words that obscure or misrepresent the real personal attitude is immoral. Casuistry had flourished in the time of Jesus through convenient formulas, cleverly constructed, but the Master taught, in the passage under discussion, that the integrity of the person under the sway of the Father would be such that no formula of appeal could surpass in effectiveness the plain Yes or No. Oaths minister to no social security; they actually give rise to misunderstanding and wrong, hence are moral outlaws.

In the ancient law of retaliation, human nature

---

[62] Matt. 22. 30.

[63] But see discussion of Divorce, pp. 184ff. below.

found itself so thoroughly intrenched that it praised the emphasis put upon it by the contemporary teacher. But this law was and is psychologically and sociologically wrong. In any community where the law of tooth for tooth, life for life, prevails there must ensue a high development of the ugly and animal in behavior. The law of retaliation is utterly unsuited to become a constructive community rule.

Jesus deliberately substituted, according to this evangelist, for the ancient and revengeful law, a rule of nonresistance. This is a constructive rule, in that it tends to develop those finer qualities which the law of retaliation would suppress. Through its adoption as a community rule, all would doubtless gain in happiness. By its adoption on the part of some only,[64] the disciples of the older law might gain some material goods from those who practiced the non-resistance rule, but the Teacher would say that the life is more than its nourishment and the body itself is more than the clothes that adorn it. It is yet to be demonstrated that all material loss is real loss or that all material goods won are real gain. Whatever the immediate consequences of Jesus' rule of nonresistance, it is clear that it is morally constructive, personally disciplinary and empowering. In plain words it says: The righteousness that surpasses that of the contemporary teachers of religion adopts a procedure which reenforces the moral power of the community, even if some material loss is met by the individual. For

[64] The Kingdom is assumed to exist within communities where all are by no means its citizens. Hence social relations between those who are within and those who are without.

to insist upon one's rights is subtly but surely to develop selfishness. And selfishness is alien to the spirit of the Reign of God.

In the last illustration, 5. 43-48, the evangelist has found Jesus' highest and finest appeal, as well as his most incisive statement of the higher righteousness. It is, in reality, "becoming sons of the Father,"[65] that is, partaking more and more of the Father's nature.

This pericope, 5. 43-48, not only constitutes the climax of the exposition in answer to the implied question, "What is the exceeding righteousness?" but it furnishes a key to the understanding of the Kingdom of heaven in the milieu of the first-Gospel writer. The Kingdom is a program of moral advance, in which men engage while they are citizens of this world. God himself is ethical in his attitude toward men, as the prophets made clear. He is not revengeful, else men had perished off the earth. Among men it has been normal, conventional to hate the unlovely, to requite damage and discourtesy, but the community suffers from such practice. In the effective, constructive moral community the surpassing test of cooperation is that of one's ability to imitate the Father and thus demonstrate the possession of filial nature. Filial nature is expressed in filial conduct. All men engaged in such high moral achievements are becoming more and more sons of the Father. The climax of the high appeal of this section reads: "Ye therefore shall be perfect, as your heavenly Father is perfect."

---

[65] The verb here (5. 45) is properly translated "become," not "be," as in most versions.

ACCORDING TO MATTHEW

Assignments for Class Reports

1. How should the ethical teaching of this chapter in Matthew be summarized?
2. What evidence is found in this part of the Sermon to indicate that Jesus broke summarily with Judaism? Is there evidence to the contrary? (See Assignment 8 p. 87.)
3. In what way did Jesus become familiar with the contemporary teaching of the scribes?
4. What is the teaching of Mark as to the "authority" of Jesus?
5. Gather together the data in this chapter (Matt. 5) which show that in the evangelist's thought the Kingdom is to be on earth.
6. Find and report upon characteristic instances of Jewish casuistry.
7. What other commandments from the Decalog might Jesus have used to illustrate the "higher righteousness"? Point out the line upon which one of such commandments might have been used.
8. In what way, if any, does the law of the present day take cognizance of a criminal intention which is not carried out in deed?
9. Judging from your knowledge of psychology, what would be the practical effect of a policy of nonresistance which should be adopted unanimously by the Christian group in a given community?

The Sermon on the Mount: Social Evidences of the Reign of God

The sixth chapter of Matthew treats of that phase of ethics taught by Jesus, which the evangelist interprets as social, and as evidential of the moral life that is bound up in motive, attitude, and intention.

On the one hand,[66] there are conventional forms, which are rooted in experiential values. Philanthropy, prayer, and fasting may, indeed, exist as forms, but the love of needy (even if unlovely) fellow men, the instinctive desire and impulse to commune with God, interest, and even absorption in any high endeavor are accompanied by if not, indeed, induced by the spiritual attitude which deprecates ostentation. Much of religion in its formal observance becomes thus ethically conditioned.

On the other hand, within the social order, property and material wealth of many kinds have real values. What effect upon these values will the Reign of God have? The new order is quite obviously of this world, for it is bound up inextricably with human activities. The answer of Jesus[67] involves the direct influence of the Kingdom upon the use of these material things and their necessary subordination to other values, those of personality, of character development, which attention to the material has too often obscured. But just as surely as the Kingdom has its place in this life of men, so surely has the Kingdom a policy in regard to wealth, economic processes, daily sustenance, and the conservation of the citizen's peace of mind.

A paraphrase of the chapter[68] will present these two aspects of the Reign of God in its social evidences:

> The essence of acceptable philanthropy is to be found in the love of men rather than the love of publicity. In the Reign of God the

[66] 6. 1–18. [67] 6. 19–34. [68] Matthew 6.

love of one's brother is a compelling motive.

Prayer, in the Kingdom, is a personal relation, not designed to attract public attention. It is the Father who hears in secret, not the public, which may be impressed but superficially, who completes the relation involved in prayer. Pray for men, not to men. Not many words, but a deep-felt need, constitutes a rewarding prayer.

Pray to your Father, for the progress of the Kingdom program. He knows your daily needs. But your other needs do not forget, your need of the filial spirit in dealing with your fellowmen.

Fasting is customary, but too often perfunctory. Even if you fast entirely in secret, washing your face and combing your hair, the community will still know, through your earnest service, rather than through a disheveled appearance, that you are a son of the Father.

Do not amass that kind of wealth that is subject to deterioration; but discern and amass values that are not subject to corruptive influences. For your greatest interest will lie in that realm where your most highly prized possessions are. As the proverb has it, generosity is like a good eye that lights the body. Use material goods so that they will be a constructive force, for otherwise, as the proverb goes, your eye is evil, and all is darkened, obscured.

It is a true principle that divided allegiance is impossible. Your chief interest cannot be placed upon competing objects. So these two kinds of values, material and personal, are mutually exclusive.

In view of all this, I assure you that the son of his Father will not suffer need. Food, raiment, housing—these are all needful for you in this life, and the Father does not forget your needs. Within the Kingdom, anxious thought and fretful worry are unfilial and alien. Even nature is cared for abundantly.

The pagan and materialist think first of things, but in the new order the Reign of God comes first, with its "exceeding rightness." Material things take their place, but it is a subordinate place.

Live a day at a time. If it is unfilial to worry about to-day's need, surely no son of the Father will borrow trouble in advance.

In summing up the ethical teaching of Matthew in the two parts of this chapter, the student will note that the bond between ethics and religion is indissoluble. Whether on the side of religious observance or on the side of a correct estimation of community values, the new order taught by Jesus is ethico-religious.

The cup of cold water given to a man in need is philanthropy. The act gains nothing if it is cleverly staged to attract public applause. On the contrary, the exhibition of self-interest may bring to the merciful act a serious depreciation. The souls surprised by their award at the great assize,[69] cried out incredulously, "When did we see thee in need and ministered to thee?" When the phil-

---

[69] Matt. 25. 37.

anthropist loves his fellow more than the applause of the crowd he is indeed letting his other hand go on its way unknowing.

Merely formal prayer lacks ethical value. How shall the community be lifted in any way if the one who prays thinks only of his own elevation on a wave of publicity? Secrecy in prayer is appropriate, not for its own sake, but because invited publicity invalidates the prayer itself.[70]

In the formal exercise of fasting the evangelist finds a striking illustration of the tendency to superficiality, ostentation, and negation of constructive value. Men who "disfigure their faces, to put on the appearance of fasting,"[71] even if they actually go through with the self-denial, thereby preempt all possibility of efficiency in any social reaction. "Truly indeed, they are receiving their pay." A reward that consists of the satisfaction of even a religious vanity is quite empty of ethical value.

But a deep-seated interest in moral endeavor or any constructive task involving community or personal service is fasting indeed, accompanied, as it often is, by self-deprivation of leisure, of amusement, of luxury, or food.

In the last part of the sixth chapter,[72] the subject changes from the inner spirit of formal religious exercise to the spirit that actuates the worthy member of the new order in his estimate of material and personal values relatively.

---

[70] The Lord's Prayer is offered by the evangelist as a model of the effective prayer. At this point it is not thought desirable to enter into its detailed exposition.

[71] 6. 16. [72] Verses 19-34.

No evidence is found to indicate the evangelist's condemnation of wealth as such. He does not appear to understand that Jesus would banish material wealth. For not only Matthew, but all the evangelists seem to understand that Jesus taught his disciples that the Reign of God was to be among men who live in the contemporary civilization and under current economic conditions. The teaching of Jesus which the First Evangelist presents here is that material values are inadequate as a chief dependence and they are perilous as objects of chief emphasis,[73] while they are subordinate to other values which are designated figuratively as "treasures in heaven," yet which are very obvious to the discerning eye in the ethical community. The evangelist knows that the ethical thought of his time took cognizance of the use of material things.[74]

The Oriental expression for niggardliness or meanness is "an evil eye,"[75] and this, as well as its opposite, "the healthy eye," appears in an exhortation to generosity in Matt. 6. 22–23. Matthew's understanding of the saying differs somewhat from Luke's, but in this exposition the evangelist is probably reminded of his former remarks upon philanthropy,[76] and pursues the subject, possibly

---

[73] Note Luke's method of teaching this, in his parable of the Rich Fool (12. 16–21). This man was not condemned because the generous attitude of God (Matt. 5. 45) had made his fields bring forth with unusual abundance, but because the fellow could not see any other than material values in life.

[74] 1 Cor. 8. 8; Rom. 14. 14ff.; also for the early church, see Acts 2. 44–46; 5. 2ff.

[75] On the "good eye" see Prov. 22. 9, margin; on the "evil eye," see Matt. 20. 15; Mark 7. 22; Deut. 15. 9; Prov. 23. 6; Sirach 14. 10.

[76] 6. 1ff.

with an implicit question as to the use of wealth in mind.

Thus the interpretation of 6. 22–23 to mean that the "exceeding righteousness" comprehends an attitude and practice of generosity is in harmony with a view shared by all the Gospel writers, and is echoed in Matt. 19. 21, as well as in the places above cited.

The law adduced in verse 24 is not arbitrary. It is based upon human nature as it is found. No man can serve two masters. The law is grounded in the essential unity of the person.[77]

The conclusion of the chapter brings to discussion a practical question which is clearly implicit in the reader's mind. The son of the Father lives in a sociological community and he is, as well, a member of that other community of those who, like him, are "becoming sons of the Father" in the sense of higher development of the Father's nature within them. This latter community is the Reign of God, or, as this evangelist has it, "the Kingdom of the heavens," and is without the clearly defined lines of demarcation that the sociological community has. Will there not be, possibly, such a conflict between the demands of the two kinds of community that the member of both will suffer? It is a fair question. The evangelist believes that the reader is entitled to its answer. And it may be that in the original discourse, Jesus spoke these words in about this order.

---

[77] That the principle was early discerned in the moral development of Israel is seen in the contest at Mount Carmel, 1 Kings, 18. 21–24, when Elijah used the exhortation, "If Jehovah be God, then follow him; but if Baal, then follow him."

The connective "therefore" in verse 25 denotes that the assurance of the Father's solicitous and ample care for his children,[78] is logically related to all that precedes. The high point in this passage is verse 33, "Seek first the Reign of God," and the type of character that such a regime demands, and all else will follow.

The flowers, the birds and the grass are illustrations of bountiful provision within nature. But within the personal realm, far more important than the lower orders of creation, the Father's care is supreme.

Character-building stands first. The body will fail at last, but a man is more than body. Something outlasts the material, and that is, in Jesus' estimation, eternally of worth. One's needs are pressing, but one's character is essential. Freedom from consuming care allows primary interest in moral endeavor, personal service, which in turn displace all those petty and often vicious worries which corrode not only this day's life but the hope of the morrow.

Assignments for Class Reports

1. What ethical teaching can be found in the Lord's Prayer?
2. What is a moral equivalent of fasting?
3. From your study of the Sermon thus far, what do you conclude as to the evangelist's attitude toward commerce and finance as desirable elements in a Christian civilization?
4. What difference, if any, would the existence of organized social work make in the First Evangelist's

[78] Verses 25–34.

teaching as to philanthropy? Were there any Associated Charities in the first century A. D.?

5. In your own words state what you understand by the evangelist's phrase, "treasure in heaven." Make your answer as specific as possible.
6. What other conventional religious forms did Judaism have besides philanthropy, prayer, and fasting?
7. Gather the data thus far presented in the Sermon about "reward." Is the expectation of reward counted an important moral sanction?
8. In what way does chapter 6 (Matt.) strengthen the view that the Reign of God is to be upon earth, among human conditions?
9. Does the Sermon thus far indicate whether the Kingdom is to be nationalistic or universal?

The Sermon on the Mount: Reciprocity Within the New Order Other Practical Tests

The first twelve verses of Matthew 7 present the evangelist's exposition of the principle of reciprocity between fellow members of the Kingdom, with probable application to those "without." In presenting his views upon reciprocity he has quoted Jesus upon judgment or criticism of one another, and this leads to further details as to moral judgments which the members of the Kingdom must make.[79] This, in turn, suggests words current in the church tradition regarding the Last Judgment,[80] following which the Sermon is concluded with the illustration of the two builders. Verses 13–14 form a transition from the ideal rule of reciprocity (the Golden Rule) to the details of discriminating

[79] 7. 15–20. [80] 7. 21–23.

judgment. The verses themselves are taken, as indeed is true of practically all the Sermon, from the relatively large number of Jesus' words that had come down to the evangelist's time in various ways and in different combinations. The admonition of 7. 13f., "Enter in at the strait gate," is probably suggested to the writer by his use of verse 7, "Knock and it shall be opened."

A paraphrase of verses 1–23 follows:

Critical judgments are infectious and at the best result but in measure for measure. Many such judgments are made blindly, and in any event conduce to no progress. Helpful judgment is possible if one make sure of the right spirit.

Some judgments are truly necessary, and those who themselves see clearly refrain from incongruous mingling of highest values with lowest.

In the Kingdom there prevails a real spirit of reciprocity, so ask and receive, strive and attain, knowing the generosity and good will of the Father, who knows so fully what to give to his children when they ask.

In the spirit of this higher reciprocity, and in denial of the spirit of captious criticism or even condemnation, look about you and after the measure of your own desire, your own need, which your Father so bountifully supplies, do you impart to other men in like generous measure. This rule of the Kingdom is in reality the spirit of the Jewish morality as found in the law and the prophets.

But the new order of society, the Reign of

God, in which such surpassing reciprocity rules, is not easily entered. The gate is not wide, one must indeed seek and knock. But it is the narrow gate that leads to life, the broad and apparent way that leads to loss.

If one must take such care then, there will be those who pretend they are under the Reign of God but who are not really of that community. For it is the inner nature that validates the life, not an assumed exterior.

Judgments must be made, the false prophet avoided, the good tree recognized by its wholesome fruit.

Tests are made at length, when the inner nature, however concealed for a time, must appear plainly. If the wolf in sheep's clothing deceive the community for a time, yet his hypocrisy is open to the Judge of all men. So the Kingdom is not a rule according to appearance, but a rule founded on transformation of character.

The question is bound to be asked by those who are learning of the new order: Who is within and who is without? What are the tests of membership? The seventh chapter of Matthew contains some answers to these inquiries, and some elaboration of the tests involved.

Some preceding words may have left the impression in the disciples' minds that in the exercise of a policy of non-resistance they are to become passive in their attitude toward those "without." But here the disciples are instructed, the evangelist says, in the mode of moral judgments. Judgment, as such, leads to retaliatory judgment. **As in 5.**

36ff. retaliation was shown to be a destructive community force, so here, blind judgment leads to a vicious circle of condemnatory criticisms. But there is a necessity for making positive moral judgments, for instance, as the disciples shall go out upon their various missions.

Matthew writes in a time when the "false prophet" was probably a distinct menace, hence the special advice[81] in his case, in further exposition of Jesus' words: "Do not judge lest you yourself be judged." The swine and pearls of 7.6 represent a moral judgment which the disciple must make. These are constructive as all laws of the Kingdom guarantee.

Judgment, then, may be actuated by different spirits. The spirit of the son of the Father guarantees constructive judgment, but that spirit needs itself to be constantly put to the test. Perhaps all the evangelists felt the force of this, for[82] at times the disciples themselves showed such inaptitude in making judgments as to merit rebuke from their Master.

All judgment that is constructive must be made according to the inner law of the Reign of God. This law involves the nature of the disciple, which is the nature of the Father. "Not every one who says to me, Lord, Lord, ... but he who does the will of my Father." The evangelist does not need to repeat here what he has said about generosity toward those who are froward and about loving the unlovely. But this is the standard for the Father's behavior and can be alone the standard for the son.

---

[81] 7. 15. [82] Mark 9. 38–41; Luke 9. 49f.

Consult human nature again, he says in substance, and discover that it waxes strong in its less lovely aspects when fed upon revenge or upon return in kind. If critical judgments are made which are first of all based upon inadequate knowledge (the mote and the beam), and in addition are ill-motived, this will but set up a train of retaliatory acts of censoriousness. The Kingdom program is constructive, hence no son of the Father will judge thus.

Moral distinctions do not in consequence lie in a gray haze. The same English word "judgment" describes these desirable acts of discernment. The expression twice adduced by the evangelist, "By their fruits shall you discern them,"[83] is a hint to the disciple to look below the surface, to scan motive behind action.

The climax of the pericope is found in the verse popularly known as the Golden Rule: "Therefore, everything which you would have men do for you, do you yourselves for them; for this is the law and the prophets."

"Therefore" indicates logical deduction from the preceding, hence it is correctly taken as the supreme statement of the kingdom-principle of consideration for others. It does not close the discussion of reciprocity, for there are particularly the illustrative sayings in 7. 15–23, but verse 12 is nevertheless the conclusion.

The specific teaching of 7. 1–12, as Matthew arranges the material, is that men of moral insight have this in common, that an unselfish or altruistic mode of looking at things provides a motive for interest in and consideration for the affairs of one

[83] 7. 16, 20; compare 12. 33.

another. This high motive finds its way into the human view from the Father, who is himself generous and kind. The principle is withal rational and constructive, thus justifies itself. A man who has such insight and experience tends to measure his service to others by his own estimate of his desire and need. Selfishness in this way suffers a certain check by becoming a measure for its own undoing. And the older Scriptures uphold the principle, for it is the teaching of the law and the prophets.

The evangelist will resume his discussion of moral criteria in the Kingdom in verse 15, but before doing so, quotes a short passage of two verses[84] concerning the two gates, one narrow, leading "into life," which forms the antithesis of "destruction," into which leads the "roomy way" of verse 13.[85]

Verses 13–14 have the same imperative form that is found in verses 1, 5, 6, 7, 12, and 15, so finds itself in no way out of harmony with the character of adjacent sayings. As is frequently the case in the Sermon, the statement of a high principle seems to suggest to the writer certain possible questions in the minds of his readers, which he will answer in so far as he can anticipate them. Upon the announcement of the Golden Rule, one of the highest points in the Sermon, the implicit question seems to be: Is this a practicable rule? or, How can one expect men to measure so high?

The admission of the evangelist is: It is indeed high, but there are words of Jesus which make

[84] 7. 13f.

[85] Luke 13. 24 uses this saying in quite a different context, where it appears much more at home. This, however, does not release the interpreter from the task of finding, if possible, the sense of the saying in the context of the First Evangelist.

answer: The program here set forth is not easy. The way of him who would become competent is, to use a common figure, entered by a narrow gate. This requires effort and search on the part of all who enter.

To the evangelist it appears as though the few would make this effort, while the many would take the obvious way. Later Christian writers have made similar statements.

The connection of verses 13–14 with the following passage seems difficult to trace. Verses 15–23 further illustrate the possible instances of moral judgments that meet the disciple. But throughout the pericope, 7. 1–23, including verses 13–14, the principle of antithesis is so abundantly used as to unify the thought somewhat.

The chapter, thus far, reveals the evangelist's understanding of Jesus' moral program in certain practical particulars. The program involves a high consideration for others, on the part of each member of the community. There will always be give and take in life, but the way of selfish regard is not the way of community-building nor of character-building. Temptations to relax diligence in such a program are pictured in the figure of the way of least resistance. The new program is, after all, the old brought into new perspective, for the law and the prophets really taught the same principle.

The Kingdom is not coextensive with the inhabited world, although it is of the world that now is. There are "false prophets," "corrupt trees," "thorns," "thistles," and "ravening wolves." These antitheses, however, guarantee the validity of the good tree and its fruit, of the path that really leads to life, though that life be conceived of as the life that men should live together in this world.

Assignments for Class Reports

1. What instances can be found in chapter 10 (Matt.) where the disciple is called upon to make moral judgments?
2. Is the Golden Rule specific or general? If only a form, how can content be put into it?
3. Do you find evidence in this chapter that the Kingdom is thought of as outside the inhabited world? Is there any evidence to the contrary?
4. Point out a practicable way in which the Golden Rule could be used in making a treaty at the close of a war for conquest.

Summary of the Ethical Content of the Sermon on the Mount

The conclusion of the sermon, Matt. 7. 24–27, is in the form of a parable:

> Two men propose to build. One of these is not farsighted, is anxious to realize upon his efforts, cannot imagine the rise of other than present conditions, hence does not expend much labor upon the foundation, which, after all, is not a very visible part of the edifice. But the storms, floods, and other destructive forces become impartial judges of his work. He loses.
>
> His counterpart is a builder who foresees untoward conditions, who calculates shrewdly, who counsels with men of experience, and compares his own experience and observation with theirs. His building rests, therefore, upon a solid foundation, either well chosen or labo-

riously constructed. The storms, winds, and other forces of nature leave him secure after their test of his work and he congratulates himself upon his consistent plan. His house becomes his secure residence.

The lesson is not left to the deduction of the reader. For the evangelist quotes the words of Jesus: "Every one who hears . . . and does, . . . shall be compared to a wise man."[86]

But the man who built for the time being, for appearance, optimistic, and perhaps saying jauntily, "The house appears secure, it will stand!" is declared to be like the foolish man. He lost his labor.

The lesson of the Two Builders applies to the entire Sermon in its present literary form. It is reading too much into the parable to say that it teaches the loss of a soul. For here in the conclusion, Jesus is more conservative in his statement than in 5. 22, where the man who calls his brother a fool incurs at least the risk of Gehenna.

Jesus has in mind the man who is evangelized. This man has heard the good news of the imminence of the new order. Practical principles of character-building, of community redemption, of conservation of life, of discernment of values, of social amity have been set forth before him. This evangelized man, this instructed soul, is irrational indeed if he chooses the lesser values, if he desires no permanency of fine character, if he forgets the vision.

The concluding illustration contains more than a

---

[86] 7. 24.

hint of the important principle expounded within the discourse, of the unseen but potent springs of action that make valid the outer life of a man.

Any summary of the Sermon on the Mount should be cast in the personal form rather than in abstract terms. In its literary form as it stands the Sermon retains much of the force and picturesqueness of the spoken address. The man, and not the multitude, was in the eye and thought of the speaker, as Matthew has brought the discourse to his readers. This "man of the Sermon" is of course the "wise man" of the conclusion. He is the composite character of the Beatitudes, the contestant who enters the lists against the "scribes and Pharisees" with the "exceeding righteousness" as his goal. He is the "son of his Father in heaven" at least potentially. He is "becoming" a son. This man belongs to the community where religious forms have often been empty, but he now cherishes the form the more because it has been enriched in content. It no longer needs to be public, for the spirit of service is more than the conventional form. This man knows more about values than he knew before. He understands that the greatest values are most enduring, not corruptible, but yet they are not as obvious as the much sought but temporary and corruptible values. This "wise man" knows too that the Reign of God guarantees the bountiful care of the Father, who knows what the son has need of before a petition is offered. He trusts the Father who anticipates his wants and achieves a peace and satisfaction of mind which enables him to put his chief efforts upon the day's work. Such a man will deal sympathetically, kindly, generously with his fellows, for his example is the Father. He will not be irrational in his passivity, but he will not be unbrotherly in any aggression. He will not put emphasis upon his own rights, which may become his brother's "wrongs," nor will he engage in any activity that will encourage the growth of selfishness. Better suffer wrong than to be wrong. Thus, retaliation and revenge offer broad avenues into the field of selfish ends. But to enter this field at all is but to deny development to the unselfish and altruistic motives. This, in turn, will make a man a negative or even destructive force in his community. No social redemption through any selfish program! He sees that if all men become thus champions of their own rights, if they develop cunning in obtaining their rights, plus all that a selfishness, easily excited, will demand, the community will serve as a prey to the long-headed plotters, and the community will be exploited, not redeemed. The wise man sees too that the spoils of the strong in this case are not enduring values to them, for the final parable of the Teacher shows the loss of that short-sighted man's work. It is the wise man, after all, who, though he is laying up for himself "treasure in heaven," is himself the greatest asset the community of men here on earth has, for he represents and wields the real power to redeem human society.

Assignments for Class Reports

1. What appropriateness is found in the selection by Jesus of the story of the Two Builders? Cite other gospel stories about building.
2. Compare the form of the concluding parable in Luke

6. 48f., and state any differences you find in literary effectiveness and in application.

3. How closely are standards of test and promise of reward related in the Sermon? How does this compare with modern ethical thought?
4. Does Jesus, according to Mark and Matthew, seem to imply that the immoral man owes his immorality to some "inner spring"?
5. Make an attempt to formulate the teaching as to ethical salvation as found in the Sermon.
6. How do modern writers on ethics estimate and graduate motives? Consult Martineau, *Types of Ethical Theory*, Vol. ii, p. 266, for his Table of Motives. Also note criticism of same in Sidgwick: *The Methods of Ethics*, p. 369. Does Jesus appear to indicate any such gradation?
7. What distinction can be made between the strictly Jewish ethics and the strictly Christian ethics represented in the Sermon?
8. Can you classify the ethics of Matthew in chapters 5–6–7 as social? as individual? If divided, which predominates?
9. At the conclusion of your study of the Sermon on the Mount, offer your statement of its theme. (Compare p. 87, Assignment 1.)

The Normative Power of the Inner Life

If behavior (conventional practice) within the community made up of those who are seeking to realize the best in life is to be constructive, conservative of personal values and weaving all the strands of public and private interests into a real brotherhood, how is this to be attained? Two ways at least may be thought of: (1) the imposition upon the community of a predetermined standard of conduct, through some form of agreement; or (2) the attainment of a relatively uniform standard of conduct which is itself determined by the individual's possession of chastened desire, high aims, disciplined impulses, and, in general, a thought-life rather free from unworthy elements. According to the First Evangelist, Jesus takes the second alternative.[87]

Without theorizing, Jesus is represented as explaining to the disciples in chapter 15 of Matthew some words which he has just spoken to the religious leaders, in the person of certain Pharisees.[88] The power to produce an ethical behavior of effective and constructive standard is the spirit of a man, itself under the power of a controlling force other than the man himself but closely identified with him. The teaching is not new in chapter 15, for it appeared in the Sermon on the Mount. A paraphrase of the address in brief form will set before the reader its essential teaching:

> In a conversation with the most exacting traditionalists of Judaism one day, the latter complained to Jesus that his disciples ate without the proper ablutions, thus setting an example of contempt for established custom.[89]
>
> Jesus countered by saying that certain established customs themselves showed contempt for the original Word of God, and quoted from

---

[87] Mark also understands that Jesus emphasized the normative power of the thought-life. See Mark 7 and compare Chapter 2, pp. 23–25, above.

[88] Matt. 15. 1–9.

[89] The Pharisees and their scribes were by far the most severe in their interpretation of the law. For an early Christian estimate of this, see Acts 26. 5, "the strictest group."

the prophet Isaiah to the effect that hundreds of years before substitution of tradition for revelation provided a superficial morality, of which the prophet justly complained.

Then Jesus turned from these particular controversialists, and addressed the people as follows:

The matter in dispute is really simple. Real evil comes from an evil mind, not through ceremony. These food laws are not moral laws. No moral deterioration comes from without.

The disciples spoke up: Do you know, Master, that the Pharisees seriously mistook your meaning? Yes, said Jesus, they do not see, for they are blind leaders. They cannot stand the test of life. Whereupon Peter said: We, at any rate, would like to understand the matter. Jesus replied: It is food that enters from without, and this is digested and disposed as nature best knows how. But think of the evils that can come out of a man, all that arise from evil thoughts, all the sinful deeds known. Compare the defilement of these evils with an unwashed hand at table![90]

As in Mark 7, this discourse is given before Pharisees, the multitude and the disciples in order, although the disciples were of course, present from the first. It is essentially disciple instruction, as the Sermon on the Mount was understood by Matthew to be. Thus, in the evangelist's exposition of the ethics of Jesus, this chapter contributes to

[90] Matt. 15. 1–20.

the reader's understanding of the ethical theory prevalent in the evangelist's time.[91]

Jesus had already been in conflict with the Pharisees over the Sabbath,[92] and this had given rise to a plot against him. On this occasion,[93] although these Pharisees were probably not the same ("from Jerusalem"), they were not looking for instruction, while the disciples were seeking to know. Although one cannot be sure of the chronological order of events in any Gospel, in both Mark and Matthew this instance of teaching is placed very near the scene at Cæsarea Philippi,[94] when Jesus was on the point of going to Jerusalem on his last fatal journey.

The pericope represents teaching that had been presented before, but still the disciples had the conventional ethics of Judaism too plainly before them. Perhaps their awe of the contemporary official teachers was still somewhat in evidence,[95] and they would thus be held under the influence of their authority. But these disciples had at least been courageous enough to follow Jesus' example and cast off the shackles of the old custom. It was the Master's protest against form as such, not against form that was expressed from inner enlightenment.

The words to the disciples are those of a serious, earnest man, penetrating below the surface of shallow and well-nigh superstitious moral instruction, showing his hearers that the life of men

---

[91] It is certain that this theory of the inner norm did not originate in the First Evangelist's time, for it forms a part of the tradition that came to Mark, perhaps a score of years earlier. It bears marks of originality, genuine Jesus-teaching.

[92] 12. 1–13. [93] 15. 1ff.

[94] Matt. 16. 13ff.; Mark 8. 27ff. [95] 15. 12.

in its deeper and most real aspects is, in fact, the field of ethics, the arena of moral forces, the valid source of the good or evil in society.

Assignments for Class Reports

1. In what part of the Sermon on the Mount is teaching similar to that in chapter 15 (Matt.) found? What differentiates this chapter from the passage in the Sermon, (*a*) in content, (*b*) in clarity?
2. What words of the Pharisees (Matt. 15. 1ff.) imply that Jesus was considered a regular member of the Jewish church?
3. What is meant by "the tradition of the elders"?
4. Search through the addresses and sermons in the book of Acts and report whether the apostles incorporated the teaching of this chapter in their public exposition.
5. After an examination of Romans 14, do you conclude that in the time of Paul (cir. 55) the teaching of Matthew 15 was current in the church?
6. Compare the parallel passage in Mark (7. 1–23) and note differences. Is the ethical teaching the same in each case? Does the addition of Matthew's "whatsoever enters into the mouth" (15. 17) make this a specific attack upon Jewish food laws?
7. What is the particular evasion of the law referred to in Matt. 15. 5?
8. To what extent do these words of Jesus (chapter 15) indicate that all traditional forms are unethical and to be abandoned?

The Brotherhood of the Kingdom: Its Mutual Ethical Relations

The eighteenth chapter of Matthew has been called the "Constitution of the Kingdom of God." Within this chapter the evangelist has gathered into a discourse of 613 Greek words, interrupted only once (verse 21) by a question from Peter, a number of paragraphs which he applies to the exposition of some most vital principles within the new moral order.

He begins with the discussion among the Twelve as to who should be greatest,[96] which Mark had given in greater detail,[97] following Mark in the saying about offending one of those who believe, and in the figurative saying about cutting off an offending member,[98] but with 18. 10, the First Evangelist adduces still other sayings to amplify his exposition. From the first Gospel, then, can be gained a fuller (and later) Christian view of the ethical community which its writer calls the "Kingdom of the heavens."

The paraphrase of 18. 10–35 offered below will present the essential Matthaean features of the Christian brotherhood.[99] It will be recalled that in 18. 1ff. the narrative concerned the question of the disciples as to who was greatest in the Kingdom.

> Do not look down upon the little ones, for their spiritual relation with the Father is direct and open. It is not, after all, for the prominent, but for the neglected that the Son of man serves. A simple tale will illustrate this:
>
> A man with a hundred sheep, one of them lost, will place his thought and effort upon the one that has strayed. The Father does not ask about the "great" alone; he will not have the "least" come to grief.

[96] 18. 1–5. [97] Mark 9. 33–37, see above, pp. 29ff.
[98] Matt. 18. 6–9; Mark 9. 42–48.
[99] The student should recall the substance of footnotes 34 and 36 on pp. 30–31 above.

So between you within the Kingdom; make every effort to keep your relationships amicable, for otherwise you may lose a brother. Be not easily discouraged if your attempts at reconciliation fail, get help from others, even from all the other brothers. Then if he persists, he will number himself among those without.

All the relationships between men of the Kingdom on earth are ratified with the Father. Thus your responsibility is infinite.

Another very important truth lies in the effectiveness of united effort, of united purpose. Two thus united have prevailing influence with the Father. Every united company of believers in the world have also my company.

Then Peter asked how patient one should be with a brother who tested one's patience frequently. Peter suggested seven times as a possible measure. But Jesus multiplied that again, not by seven, but by seventy, without further comment, except to relate a story, as follows:

The Kingdom is comparable to the king who examined the accounts of his servants, in particular with two of them. The first owed him, it seems, such a sum that he could never possibly pay it. So the law was invoked and an order given to sell him and his family in payment of the debt. The debtor made such an effective plea, however, that his lord's sense of personal loss was changed to mercy and he actually forgave the man all his debts. Thereupon the forgiven debtor hunted up a man who owed him a small sum and insolently demanded full payment. All this debtor's prayers availed not, and he was cast into prison. When the report of his unmerciful act reached the king, however, the mercy of the latter turned to strict justice and he cast the fellow into prison to remain indefinitely. Jesus closes his story with a statement that the Father also would requite men who did not find it in their hearts to forgive their fellows.

It should be noted that this teaching is late in the life of Jesus, as the evangelist places it after the Transfiguration and just before the last journey to Jerusalem.[100] It is disciple-instruction, as most of the teaching of Jesus in this Gospel is.

The words are clearly thought by the evangelist to constitute some of the parting words of Jesus with the Twelve as to their program after he should leave them. Note the mention of the Master's presence with them,[101] where even "two or three are assembled." Their program will continue "on earth"[102] and the relations of amity and cooperation between them would be chief among the elements of their success. In the evangelist's day he could look back upon many instances which verified this.[103]

The ethical substance of the address is clear. The Reign of God is evidenced in the company of those who comprise its membership by relative unanimity, absence of discrimination against the so-called "least," that is, the less prominent, and every

[100] 19. 1. [101] 18. 20. [102] 18. 18, 19.

[103] Note Acts 2. 1, 46f.; 4. 32a; 1 Cor. 1. 10; Eph. 4. 25b; and similar passages that reflect conditions in the Christian community before the first Gospel was written.

typical member of the community will make unremitting efforts to maintain relations of amity with all other members. This attitude has its sanction in the attitude of the Father toward his sons who compose the community.

According to this address, it is possible, in fact, inevitable that differences will arise,[104] and that the trespassing brother may even apostatize.[105] All the normal conditions of human society are reckoned with, yet the policy of the Kingdom is to seek to modify those conditions, until the relations between men in the Kingdom and without stand out in contrast.[106]

Nothing has been adduced by the evangelist to instruct one in detail as to Jesus' theory of the inner moral nature, excepting the outstanding passage concerning the gradual development of men into "sons of the Father,"[107] and the frequent assumption of the filial relation.[108] That there was a theory of spiritual relation to or union with Jesus himself in the Christian community before this evangelist's time is known from the letters of Paul and others. It does not appear to be Matthew's purpose so much to discuss the theory of the disciples' relation to the Father and to Jesus as to state it, for example, in such a manner as 12.50, "Whosoever shall do the will of my Father in heaven, the same is my brother and sister and mother."[109]

Assignments for Class Reports

1. Note the relative number of instances in this chapter

---

[104] 18. 15; compare 5. 23; 18. 21.
[105] 18. 17. [106] 5. 45-48.
[107] Matt. 5. 45. [108] 6. 4, 6, 9, 14; 18. 15, "brother."
[109] Compare above p. 71f.

where Jesus says "my Father" and "your Father," compare this with usage in the Sermon on the Mount. What inference can be drawn?

2. Find the story of the lost sheep in Luke, parallel to 18. 12–14, and indicate what, if any, difference there is in its use and teaching.
3. Write a paraphrase of 18. 1–9.
4. In what way does 18. 15–17 explain the application of 18. 21–22? Detail the social application of this principle in the community best known to you.
5. What new note in the teaching of Jesus does 18. 35 introduce? Does it introduce any inconsistency with Matt. 12. 17–21? Do the two passages refer to the same person? Are both original with Jesus? May not one or both be adduced by the evangelist?

The Nationalism of the First Gospel

The first Gospel agrees with Mark and Luke that at some point during his Galilæan ministry Jesus sent twelve of his disciples out upon a mission which involved a proclamation of the coming Reign of God and also service on the part of the "apostles" which was distinctly social in nature.

The ground of this mission, in Matthew, is to be discovered in 9.36f., namely, in the great pity that Jesus felt for the "exploited" and "unshepherded" people whom he saw on every hand. Into this piteous and plenteous harvest he asked that the disciples pray the Lord to send laborers, which prayer they themselves answered in part by going into the villages of Galilee, healing diseases, restoring unbalanced minds, and proclaiming the near approach of the Reign of God.

Thus the mission of the Twelve arose out of a social need and theirs was a much needed task in social service. The recognition of social neglect and lack of adequate and sympathetic leadership among the peasantry of Galilee is a distinct ethical note in Matthew 10. The term "lost sheep"[110] gets its content from 9.36, thus meaning "neglected," or "without adequate social guidance and organization," rather than "lost" in a theological sense.[111]

Since the proclamation of the nearness of the Kingdom was an element in the social service of the Twelve,[112] the evangelist appears to identify healing and exorcising as part of the moral renovation implied in the coming of the Reign of God. In the economic stress which was an oppressive feature of life in Galilee, it would be indeed a positive element in social reconstruction if men hitherto dependent upon the bounty of the community became wage-earners as a result of the loss of their infirmities. This, of course, was not the extent of the missionaries' activities. The unselfish example of the disciple, trusting to the providence of God[113] and to the hospitality of the community which he served,[114] would beget other unselfish service.

The diagnosis of Jesus was not that of an enthusiastic optimist. He saw in the villages and cities inhospitable people who would not give a proper reception to one doing good,[115] and he compared the disciples to "sheep in the midst of wolves,"[116] while some of the "wolves" were identified as men

---

[110] Compare Matt. 18. 12–14.

[111] The term "neglected" is perhaps too weak to express just what the evangelist states. The student will recall that Mark (12. 38–40) found a teaching of Jesus, given at Jerusalem, which involved the scribes in practices comparable to the "flaying" or "exploiting" of the people in Galilee, as Matt. 9. 36 has it.

[112] 10. 7. [113] Matt. 5. 25–34; 10. 29–31. [114] 10. 9f.

[115] 10. 14. [116] 10. 16.

who would actually persecute and even kill the missioners.[117] Jesus' own consciousness of a social prophet's lot told him that the earnest disciple would share his own fate.[118]

The evangelist has gathered material for a discourse of some length, addressed to the Twelve as they were departing upon their mission. The whole of chapter 10 is taken up with this discourse, and the paraphrase following will indicate not only the particulars above recited, but will exhibit the strong nationalistic attitude held by the First Evangelist toward the work of Jesus. Data from other parts of this Gospel easily corroborate this statement. The address to the apostles, however, strikes the keynote of such a nationalism as prevailed within the Jewish-Christian communities of the first century.

> After calling the attention of his disciples to the distressed condition of many of the Jewish people in Galilee, Jesus took twelve of his followers, Peter, Andrew, James, John, Philip, Bartholomew, Thomas, Matthew, James, son of Alphæus, Thaddæus, Simon of Cana, and Judas Iscariot, and sent them out upon a mission, with directions to restore the sick and mentally deranged and proclaim the coming of the Kingdom.
>
> "Do not take any road that leads toward Gentile people," said Jesus, "and enter no Samaritan city. Your mission is to the lost sheep of the house of Israel.
>
> "Take no abundant provision for your needs,

---

[117] 10. 17, 19, 28. [118] 10. 24.

neither money or clothes in reserve. Depend upon the hospitality of those whom you serve. And if you find inhospitable people, or if any refuse your service, let them take the responsibility and bear the consequences of their act. I assure you, theirs will be no light penalty!

"This indicates that all men will not be friendly. You will even be brought into the courts and be scourged. But you will find yourselves unusually well equipped for defense, for the Spirit of your Father will in reality be the advocate.

"Even then, you may be brought to death. But the death of the body is a lesser calamity than to be disloyal. So fear indeed anyone or any power that can bring your soul into dishonor. To deny me, to prove unfilial indeed—this is to be feared. Be always assured of the Father's solicitude and care for you, for he watches over even the sparrows, worth so little in comparison with a man!

"It may be you will be called upon to sever family relations, but even here loyalty to your mission comes first. He who would prove worthy of me must deny himself all things that would turn him from his path, yes, he must even take his cross upon his shoulders, signifying his devotion even unto death.

"So I send you forth, to depend upon the bounty that you may receive. It will be the reward of a prophet and he who receives you will not lose his reward."

A strictly nationalistic note is struck at the opening of the discourse. The directions given would keep the apostles within Galilee. They are to go into no road leading to foreign cities and into no Samaritan city. The note struck here is quite characteristic of this evangelist, as evidenced by his insertion into the story of the Syrophœnician (Greek) woman[119] the saying, not found in Mark 7. 24–30, "I was not sent except to the lost sheep of the house of Israel." Throughout the first Gospel, much stress is placed upon the close relationship of Jesus to the Jewish people, as 2. 2, "King of the Jews";[120] 8. 11, "they shall sit down with Abraham, and Isaac, and Jacob in the Kingdom of heaven";[121] 19. 28, promise that the Twelve "shall sit upon twelve thrones, judging the twelve tribes of Israel" 21. 4f., Jesus hailed as fulfilling the prophet's word, "Say to the daughter of Zion, Lo, thy King cometh to thee."

The evangelist's strong Jewish sympathies are noted in other ways, vividly, for instance in the many instances of fulfilled prophecies, where the fulfillment satisfies a specifically Jewish hope, as 1.22f.; 12. 17ff.; 13. 35; 26. 56; 27. 9.

Further evidence of the nationalistic leaning of this writer is found in his version of the Markan account of Jesus' visit to the heathen regions where lived the Greek woman whose persistence brought healing to her daughter. In Matthew 15. 21f., Jesus goes to the boundaries of Tyre and Sidon,

---

[119] Matt. 15. 24.

[120] Compare 27. 11, Jesus' affirmative answer to the question of Pilate, "Art thou the king of the Jews?"

[121] Compare less Jewish manner of expression, Luke 13. 28f., "they shall see Abraham, and Isaac, and Jacob . . . and they shall recline in the Kingdom cf God."

but the woman "comes out" to him, thus leaving a clear impression that Jesus did not enter heathen territory.

Mark 7. 24 states with no ambiguity at all that the woman went into a house where Jesus had taken refuge, hoping to remain incognito. In his revision of the narrative of Mark, Matthew seems deliberately to conform Jesus' words to the woman to his own nationalistic restrictions.[122]

Other evidence is scarcely needed to show that as far as the First Evangelist was concerned, the mission of the Twelve, like the mission of Jesus, was for Jewish people and Jewish proselytes alone.

Assignments for Class Reports

1. To what extent does the mission of the Twelve in Matthew support the Jewish view that the Kingdom of God was essentially a regime of material good, economic reform, and Jewish supremacy?
2. What aspects of economic betterment appear in the Kingdom of God as seen by Matthew?
3. Trace the use of the term "sons of the Kingdom" throughout the first Gospel and note any variation in meaning.
4. Matt. 21. 43 represents Jesus as threatening that the Kingdom shall be taken away from the Jewish people. What historic fact known to the evangelist does this unique saying reflect?
5. What interpretation did the Twelve actually put upon the saying of Jesus in Matt. 28. 19f.? Consult the book of Acts. What one or more of the Twelve attempted any foreign mission? Compare the form of the Great Commission found in Acts 1. 8.
6. Was the ethics of Judaism nationalistic or otherwise?

[122] Matt. 10. 5f.

Consult J. M. P. Smith, *The Moral Life of the Hebrews;* and H. G. Mitchell, *The Ethics of the Old Testament.*

7. Does the First Evangelist strengthen or weaken his nationalistic view of Jesus' mission when he quotes Jesus' words, 8. 10?
8. Can one successfully justify a nationalistic ethics in the present time?

Ethics and Religion: A Study of the Ruling Classes in Judaism

An unbiased reading of Matthew 23. 2–39, a discourse containing 638 Greek words, much of which either has no parallel in the other Gospels, or contains the same matter in other words, or is expanded by the writer,[123] leaves the impression either that the First Evangelist was sure that Jesus despaired of winning the ruling classes to his following, or that the Master publicly denounced the scribes and Pharisees in very striking terms of invective, or else that the First Evangelist himself has collected, arranged, and edited words of Jesus in such a way as to exhibit the attitude of the Christian Church of his time toward these leaders.

Acts 15. 5 and the entire story of Paul reveal the existence of a considerable number of Pharisees within the church during the forties whose prestige was such that they influenced the policy of the church in certain directions. Notwithstanding this,

[123] The following verses in Matthew, 23. 2, 3, 5, 7b, 8, 9, 10, 15–22, 24, 27b, 28, 31, have no parallel in Mark or Luke. Other passages, as 23. 13, 23, 25f., 38, and others, contain significant words added by the First Evangelist, for example, "scribes," "hypocrites," "desolate" (the last with some textual doubt); which points to editing of the material by the evangelist, or to some other source. The latter is not as acceptable an hypothesis.

it must be admitted that the Pharisees and the scribes on the whole were immune to the appeal of Jesus. It must also be admitted that the total character of the first Gospel indicates that its writer was not sympathetic with the liberal tendency, as it would appear to him, of Paul and other propagandists who carried the gospel to Hellenists, but would rather side with the Pharisees of Acts 15. 5, who appear to have carried much of their conservatism with them when they entered the Jerusalem church.

There is therefore an adequate demand for a study of this chapter (23) of the first Gospel with a view to ascertaining the thought of its writer about the ethics of the leading teachers and religious classes, as well as his view of the relation between ethics and religion. Previous writers upon moral themes within Judaism had laid stress upon the fundamental character of religion as a sanction for and guarantee of a moral life.[124] Many of the reported words of Jesus likewise stress the close, well-nigh indissoluble relation between religion and morals.[125] Thus the First Evangelist would be expected to follow other Jewish writers in demanding of religious men not only the performance of regularly appointed religious services but also the possession of moral integrity which should appear in their public and private life.

The following paraphrase of Matthew 23. 1–39 will set before the student this evangelist's understanding of Jesus' arraignment of the strictest of

[124] See J. M. P. Smith, *Moral Life of the Hebrews*, pp. 137f.; 247; esp. 319.

[125] Mark 12. 38–40; Matt. 7. 21ff.; 5. 23f., and many other passages.

the religious leaders as to their fulfillment of his expectation.

Jesus addressed the people and his disciples thus: "The scribes and Pharisees took possession of Moses' seat. Where their teaching plainly is of the old moral law, follow that, but do not imitate these teachers in moral practice. Their teaching and their lives do not correspond. They are publicists, doing ostentatious things, devising burdens for others but avoiding the same themselves. They plan to get prominent places and to be called complimentary names, such as Father, Teacher and Master.

"As for you, my followers, seek no such titles. You have one Father, the heavenly Father, and Christ alone is Master. It is strange, yet true, that he who seeks exaltation must yield to him who honestly and modestly hides his goodness.

"I have a number of charges against the scribes and Pharisees, namely, that they stress nonessentials in their teaching, and that they live lives that misrepresent a true morality."

Then, apostrophizing these religious leaders and teachers, Jesus said:[126]

"Alas, for you yourselves are not entering into heaven and you prevent others from entering in.

"Alas, for you pretend by all means to bring

[126] The evangelist does not record any answer of the scribes and Pharisees to this terrible arraignment, verses 13–36, and he definitely says that the audience consisted of "the multitudes" and "disciples" (23. 1), thus the paraphrase takes a form that assumes the absence of the two classes described.

men into blessedness but you actually so teach men that they become worse than yourselves.

"Alas, blind as you are, you make false distinctions that seem real to you! Hairsplitting moralists! Dealers in casuistry! You teach men to evade the law, not to fulfill it.

"Alas, for your painful attention to the tithe of garden herbs and your glaring indifference to justice, mercy and faith! To attend to one small duty and neglect many weighty obligations is like straining out carefully the smallest mite and blindly bolting a large mass.

"Alas, for your moral example! The outside polished and fine, but within gorged with the results of extortion and graft. O blind Pharisee! The inside is more important than the outside. If you are clean within, the outside will become cleansed.

"Alas, for your very reputation! Men believe you are holy, judging from your pious veneer. Like whited graves, all bright without! But within!

"Alas, that you are self-confessed sons of those who murdered the men of God. The sepulchers of these martyrs you decorate indeed, but are preparing to send other martyrs after them! You are but repeating the history that you piously read!"

Then, apostrophizing the city itself, Jesus said:

"O Jerusalem, Jerusalem: A ruined habitation left to you, whom I would have cherished and whom I love! I go the way of all those prophets whom your pious men have stoned and killed, and you shall see me not, until that future coming! Then men shall see aright and hail him who comes in the name of Jehovah."

As the discourse appears, it represents the result of literary assembling of sayings of Jesus, originally spoken upon occasions no longer traceable, but put together here after the plan of the evangelist, who seeks, in a long discourse, to represent Jesus' attitude toward the contemporary Jewish teachers. The address may well express also the evangelist's attitude toward the Jewish teachers of morals, as was suggested above.

The most virulent part of the chapter comprises the seven "woes" spoken against the scribes and Pharisees. The paraphrase offers a modern statement of these "woes," using the term "alas"[127] to express the apparent feeling of the speaker, who will not express a malediction but wishes, rather, to record his utter dismay at the "blindness" of learned men who fail to see the work of simple moral truths so often plainly expounded before them. The scribes and Pharisees are becoming lost on their way to life, their vision taken up with the casuistry of their profession and with the trifling and puttering, dividing of mint, anise, and cummin into tenths, while the great duties of service, gracious love of their fellows, and social justice await a faithful servant.

To summarize the ethical teaching of Matthew 23, then, the evangelist emphasizes the contrast between pious profession and moral performance. He discountenances ostentation in religious exercises

---

[127] See Plummer, *Exegetical Commentary on Matthew*, p. 316f.

and scrambling selfishly for position, since these things usually indicate self-seeking rather than social love and service.

The evangelist distinctly states that Jesus warned his disciples against the assumption of titles and prerogatives for their own sake. He enjoins the humble spirit as the best safeguard against intolerant and immoral egotism.

The contemporary teachers are upon a road leading away from life. This road they blindly pursue. No hope really exists for them as a class. They proselytize but debauch the proselytes; they seek ingenious ways of evading vows, but in reality blaspheme God; they are intent on trifles and oblivious to social duty; they appear holy, but are grossly immoral; they say they would never persecute holy men as their fathers did, but they are now preparing to do even worse than they.

In the judgment of the First Evangelist, the contemporary teachers are not fairly interpreting the moral message of the past. It remained for the prophet of Galilee to do this for his generation. In opening to his people the fullness of the moral law and in showing them to the full a blameless moral life, Jesus had to come into fatal conflict with the traditionalists who blindly pursued their fateful way.

Assignments for Class Reports

1. To what extent are the "woes" of verses 13–36 symmetrical in their literary form? Compare the different English versions. Why was verse 14 not included in the American Revised Version?
2. How widely are the parallels to some of these words

scattered? Consult both Luke and Mark in the harmony of the Gospels.

3. In what way, if any, do the seven woes of Matthew 23 correspond to the Beatitudes of chapter 5? Compare Luke 6. 20–26.
4. What correspondence do you find between the immoral practices of the scribes and Pharisees in Matthew 23 and those of earlier Jewish or Hebrew people, as shown in Isa. 1. 1–23; Amos 5. 21—6. 6; Ezekiel 34? Find other Old Testament passages that reflect similar immoral conditions among the Israelites.
5. State in modern social terms the particular moral problem or problems found in Matthew 23.
6. Indicate some modern forms of casuistry.
7. What particular ethical teaching in Matthew 23 is also found in the Sermon on the Mount?
8. Who were some of the "prophets, wise men, and scribes" of verse 34? Can you verify their fate from the Bible?
9. Show whether chapter 23 is harmonious with the attitude of the Sermon on the Mount in regard to the Mosaic law.

The Ethics of the Family in the First Gospel

The thought of the First Evangelist is clearly based upon a monogamous theory of the family, and he tacitly accepts the conventional Jewish family ethics as the basis of Jesus' teaching.

John Baptist protests the legality of Herod's marriage with his sister-in-law, Herodias, on the basis of Lev. 18. 16, and in the story of the Sadducees' conversation with Jesus[128] the evangelist assumes the current assent to the levirate marriage[129] while in the story of the Nativity of Jesus,

[128] 22. 23ff. [129] Deut. 25. 5–10.

Joseph is "of a mind to divorce Mary his promised wife" under suspicion, since betrothal in Jewish circles was as binding as marriage.

In this Gospel Jesus quotes the Decalog[130] with approval and thoroughgoing interpretation of the law against adultery, although here and in 19. 3–12, the Master, according to Matthew, leans away from the provision for divorce in Deut. 24. 1–4 insofar as it has been laxly interpreted, and agrees with the stricter rabbinical interpretation of his own day, that fornication only, and that on the part of the wife, is ground for divorce.[131]

The Jewish attitude toward woman is implicit in this Gospel, in that the wife has no right to divorce her husband under any circumstances, while Mark is influenced by Roman procedure[132] in proposing the case where the wife divorces her husband.

In the first Gospel Jesus makes two pronouncements upon the moral right of divorce. In each case[133] a certain restriction is put by the evangelist upon the absolute negation of divorce. The restriction in each case concerns immorality on the part of the wife, "except for fornication,"[134] "except for the case of fornication."[135] In some of the manuscripts these phrases read identically, but in the text most generally followed in English-speaking countries,[136] they differ as above noted.

---

[130] 5. 27, compare Exod. 20. 14; Deut. 5. 18.
[131] The recent works on the divorce question by R. H. Charles, G. H. Box and others should be consulted. R. H. Charles, *Teaching of the New Testament* on Divorce, London, 1921. Box-Gore, et al., *Divorce in the New Testament.*
[132] Mark 10. 12.
[133] Matt. 5. 32 and 19. 9. [134] 19. 9. [135] 5. 32.
[136] Westcott and Hort.

Many have attempted to make plausible the theory that ecclesiastical hands placed this exception in the two Matthæan places, but all textual evidence goes to show that they are original. There is not a shred of evidence to contradict the view that the evangelist who wrote the first Gospel inserted the restriction. The question as to the originality of the phrase in either case with Jesus is one that must be deferred at least until the close of the present inductive study of the ethical teaching of the Gospels.

The student will readily recall from previous chapters that the evangelist is portraying Jesus as the announcer of the Reign of God, and that in address, conversation, and parable the Master teaches chiefly his own disciples the mode of life and character within that community of men and women striving for the most efficient moral-social order.

When Jesus defined the type of uprightness that should characterize the man of the Kingdom, he pointed out that he would do no murder if he checked the incipient hateful thought, that he would not commit adultery if he suffered no unsocial thought to develop within his soul. Thus, within the Kingdom, it would surely be the normal thing for ideal marriage relations to prevail. Hence he could urge the essential indissolubility of the marriage bond; while it is also thinkable that exceptions would occur, even within the Kingdom. For[137] the evangelist finds warrant for supposing that a brother within the Kingdom might become stubborn in his refusal to become reconciled. In this case, separa-

---

[137] Matt. 18. 15–17.

tion from the community of those who conform to the law of the Kingdom is inevitable and necessary. Such separation protects the community from contamination from within. So in the Sermon on the Mount[138] the evangelist again finds warrant for supposing that within the Kingdom a man may approach God with his gift and then recall that he has acted in a manner toward his brother which shuts him out from communion with the Father. In this case the evangelist assumes a reconciliation and the resumption of worship.

From the foregoing consideration it would not be surprising if Matthew, perhaps on the basis of his experience in the early church, correctly represented Jesus as providing for actual cases of unkingdom-like behavior within the Christian family. Even if Jesus did not himself put the case in Matthew's words, the Master offered analogies that readily justify the First Evangelist's statement of his position.

On the other hand, this evangelist offers substantial teaching as to the mutual bearing of Kingdom members toward each other, especially in chapter 18. Peter was to be ready to forgive an offending brother "seventy times seven," the farm-hands were not to tear out with ruthless hands the darnel that grew with the wheat,[139] for fear of injury to the grain. If one within the Kingdom who is not one's wife commit some offense that rankles, and one go and talk it over with the offender, it may be that one's brother will be won.[140]

It is entirely in harmony with this program of Jesus as the evangelist has set it forth, that no

[138] 5. 23–24. [139] 13. 29. [140] 18. 15f.

summary divorce action would be approved within the Kingdom. If an offending brother were worth an effort toward reconciliation, if his worth potentially warranted repeated forgiveness, if self-restraint and perseverance on the part of the offended one were amply rewarded in the winning of a brother, surely the thought of the evangelist as well as the thought of the Teacher himself would be against such summary divorce proceedings as Hillel advocated,[141] and would rather invoke the procedure of loving attempt to restore right relations and a right inner attitude on the part of offending wife (or husband either, as Mark would have it).

The word used in Matthew's exceptive clause, "fornication," connotes repeated and deliberate immorality. As a practical measure, just as Paul had taught his congregations, before this Gospel was written,[142] one who persistently remains unfaithful to any of the laws of the Kingdom has but one fate, that of exclusion. Such exclusion is not so much a judgment as it is a conservative measure. In such a regime, of course, the unfaithful married person might not remain with the faithful in intimate fellowship.[143]

The figure of the family is fundamental to Jesus' exposition of the Reign of God. The family is designed to be the emblem and source of purity within the Kingdom. Thus it is central in the moral thought of the Master and his disciples.

---

[141] This liberal rabbi interpreted the law of Deut. 24. 1–4 to mean that divorce might follow summarily upon any unhappy domestic event.

[142] 2 Cor. 6. 17f.

[143] Compare Paul in 1 Cor. 7. 12–17; 5. 9–13, for practical church procedure in the Christian Church before Matthew wrote.

Assignments for Class Reports

1. Write a short sketch upon the Jewish attitude toward woman in Jesus' time.
2. Estimate the bearing of Hosea, chapters 1–3, upon the teaching of Matthew concerning family ethics.
3. Report upon the varying interpretations of the Old Testament divorce law by Rabbis Hillel and Shammai.
4. Compare the teaching of Paul upon family ethics with the teaching of the First Evangelist upon that subject.
5. To what extent is Old Testament ethics a support to double-standard ethics? To what extent is this true of Matthæan ethics?
6. State what if any evidence exists in the New Testament to show that the Christian community acted seriously upon the teaching upon family ethics set forth by the First Evangelist.
7. What evidence appears above to show that the Kingdom is upon earth?

Reward in the First Gospel as a Sanction of Moral Endeavor

The thoroughly Jewish character of the First Evangelist is betrayed by many of his selections of sayings, and perhaps never more clearly than in his use of teaching by the Master concerning reward for leaving all and following him, for faithfulness in service and for endurance "unto the end."

So often does the idea of reward occur in this Gospel that it appears desirable to examine this aspect of the evangelist's ethics in a section by itself. The abundance of material dealing with reward, or, as the Greek expression has it, "pay," "wages," has attracted the attention of interpreters of the Gospel.[144]

In many of the sayings about "reward," either heaven is indicated as the place or the future the time of its award. "Great is your reward in heaven,"[145] "you have no reward with your Father in heaven,"[146] "treasure up for yourselves treasures in heaven,"[147] are specific references to "the heavens," used by the evangelist in the strictly Jewish sense of the abode of the Father.

The terms "eternal life," "kingdom prepared for you," and "in the kingdom of my Father" are used in a sense that differs from that in certain instances where "the Kingdom of the Heavens" or "the Kingdom of God" is found upon the lips of Jesus when he is discussing mundane and not future events. Following are a number of these sayings, in which the reward indicated is in the future and in some cases certainly at the time of judgment at the end of the world, as held by Jewish apocalypticists.[148]

"He shall be called great in the Kingdom of Heaven" (5. 19b), "and your Father who sees in secret shall reward you" (6. 4, 6b, 18), "he who

---

[144] McNeile, in his commentary on Saint Matthew, p. 54, points out a number of these passages in the first Gospel which contain thoroughly Jewish terms concerning reward at the hands of God, and in addition notes that in some words ascribed to Jesus the Jewish idea is so transformed that he "really eliminates the idea of reward." The student should follow McNeile's suggestion in the above note and consult H. B. Swete, *Apocalypse of John*, p. 306.

[145] 5. 12. [146] 6. 1. [147] 6. 20.

[148] It is not practicable to enter into a discussion of apocalypticism in its history and various developments here, but the student should become familiar with such works as *Primitive Christian Eschatology*, by E. C. Dewick; Articles in the *Dictionary of the Bible*, and such monographs as appear in the Symposium on Eschatology in the Journal of Biblical Literature, 1922, Vol. xii, pp. 102–182.

finds his life shall lose it, and he who lost his life for my sake shall find it,"[149] "then the righteous shall shine forth as the sun in the kingdom of their Father," better rendered, perhaps, "in the Reign of their Father,"[150] "when the Son of man shall sit upon the throne of his glory, you also shall sit upon twelve thrones, judging the while the twelve tribes of Israel,"[151] and "he shall inherit life eternal"[152] are characteristic passages that speak of reward in the future.

The teaching of those portions of the Gospel which have been subjected to analysis thus far gives one a decided impression that in the mind of the evangelist Jesus did not hold a brief for any form of selfishness or egotism. If, then, one is to assume that the teaching of Jesus is presented in a form believed by the Gospel writer to be consistent in every part, the reward held before the disciple offers indeed a hope of a better lot than the Master predicted in 10. 16–23, which hope may well nerve the apostle to "endure to the end."

Those who find in the language of Jesus the reflection of current views of the future are nearest correct. The evangelist himself is more in sympathy with that picture of the future which finds the faithful apostles upon twelve thrones, judging the twelve tribes of Israel, than the other Gospel-writers, who are more thoroughly under the domination of Roman and Greek ideals.

There is nothing to hinder the supposition that Jesus himself, a child of Judaism, as far as his religious training is concerned, was thoroughly con-

---

[149] 10. 39. [150] 13. 43. [151] 19. 28. [152] 19. 29b.

versant with the apocalyptic hopes of his people, and that he voiced his message in such terms as would appeal to the shepherdless and downcast sons of Israel and at the same time nerve his apostles to a sustained effort in their declaration of the good news that the Reign of God was imminent.

Other portions of the Gospel also show clearly that the Master, in Matthew's understanding of his message, emphasized personal, spiritual values as chief values, upon which the greatest emphasis should be placed. In the realm of the spiritual lie those rewards which are most enduring. "Fear not that man who can kill the body!" "Lay up those treasures which are not subject to corrosive influences!" The characteristic note in Jesus' promise of reward, in this Gospel, which emphasizes it most, is also one with his note of emphasis upon the spiritual, enduring values in life.

Reward, in Jesus' thought, is not a *quid pro quo*, but it is that type of life itself which results from sustained moral endeavor. This is indeed a sanction of moral effort. It is a rational use of the promise of rewarding fruitage in character. But it is true that for present-day readers the language itself seems to go beyond its real meaning.

Assignments for Class Reports

1. Can it be shown that the Matthæan teaching as to penalties, for example, 10. 15; 11. 24; 12. 36; 13.30f.; 15. 13; 16. 27b; 24. 48–51; 25. 41 and other passages, is couched in figurative Oriental imagery? What is the solid ethical teaching, then, under the imagery?
2. What passages in Matthew indicate that reward will be in terms of the service rendered or good deed done?

3. Paraphrase either 20. 1–16 or 25. 31–46, bringing out their moral teaching in modern terms.
4. What evidence do you find in Matthew to warrant the conclusion that the evangelist wrote particularly to encourage his readers to persevere? What evidence is there against this view?
5. In what sense do the Beatitudes hold out reward as a result of right doing?
6. How is the term "reward" to be interpreted in such passages as Matt. 5. 46; 6. 2, 5, 16b; 10. 40–42?
7. Which of the following passages contain promise of reward for right-doing: Matt. 6. 33; 7. 7–11; 10. 10b; 11. 28f.; 25. 21; 25. 28?

The Matthæan Conception of the Reign of God

The name used by the First Evangelist for the new order announced and ushered in by John Baptist and Jesus, namely, "the Kingdom of Heaven,"[153] has been taken by some to indicate that the evangelist thought of the new order as superearthly, to appear at the end of this order of things and thus to replace the earthly with the heavenly.

Such a view became very popular in certain minds several years ago and still persists as one interpretation of the Kingdom of God in the other Gospels as well as in the first Gospel. But there appear excellent reasons to suppose that in the mind of the evangelist and of Jesus, the Kingdom or Reign of God was "at hand" in a real sense for those unshepherded and downcast Israelites who so aroused the compassion of Jesus as he looked over the Galilæan

[153] Literally, "Kingdom of the Heavens."

hills. As for the name, the First Evangelist uses "Kingdom of God" in 12.28; 19. 24; 21. 31, 43,[154] and his favorite term, "Kingdom of Heaven," is no doubt the exact equivalent of "Kingdom of God" or "Reign of God."[155]

Certainly there is nothing in the Matthæan term to indicate that he thought of the new order as an extra-mundane community. The men of the Kingdom functioned as "the salt of the earth," and as "the light of the world,"[156] and their mode of maintaining brotherly relations[157] assumed their proximity to appointed places and time of worship, as well as the presence in their environment of the smaller or greater exasperating factors of social intercourse,[158] whereby their effective filial and fraternal relations were affected. Their acts of worship would be null and void as long as an unreconciled breach existed between the worshiper and his brother, and Kingdom relations became unreal if another had provoked a quarrel which the aggrieved brother refused to arbitrate. "Love your enemies"[159] is surely out of place if no enemies exist within reach, and the injunction to "lay up treasures in heaven" involves a person who has to be warned against laying up treasure "on earth," where he is assumed to live. When Jesus quotes with approval from Hosea, "I desire mercy and not sacrifice," and urges men to go and learn what

---

[154] In some MSS. 19. 24 reads "of heaven" and in some 6. 33 reads "of God."

[155] Plummer: *Exegetical Commentary on Saint Matthew*, p. 25, suggests that the form "Kingdom of heaven" more nearly meets the Aramaic original, but the other evangelists found their phrase, "Kingdom of God," more intelligible to their readers, or less liable to misunderstanding.

[156] 5. 13–16. [157] 5. 23ff. [158] 18. 15–20. [159] 5. 44.

that means,[160] and teaches that the giving of a cup of water "in the name of a disciple" is praiseworthy and rewarding, he assumes, in the understanding of the evangelist, that the principles governing life under the Reign of God are principles governing the lives of men who belong within a human environment.

Further, Jesus stressed the imminence of the Kingdom, it was "at hand,"[161] and he makes vivid his declaration that the Kingdom has indeed surprised men by its coming[162] if it be true that cures were wrought by the Spirit of God. In Matt. 4. 23–25 the threefold ministry of Jesus, "teaching . . . proclaiming . . . healing," appears to be characteristic of the Kingdom as it was being established among men.

The Reign of God has, then, much to do with the life that men live on this earth, with economic, financial, sociological, and religious as well as strictly moral affairs. The First Evangelist clearly teaches that the Reign of God applies to human beings under human conditions, even though, as also appears, he believes that this divine sway is destined to a most wonderful triumph in a future era.

Thus a future picture of the Reign of God is delineated by the First Evangelist, but the Teacher whether warning the unprepared that they will be excluded from its blessings[163] or holding before the disobedient or careless the necessity of exclusion of the unfit from the mature and harmonious society

---

[160] 9. 10–13. [161] 4. 17. [162] 12. 28.
[163] 25. 1–13; 22. 11–14.

of those who become sons of the Father,[164] or, again, reminding his hearers that the coming of the Kingdom will bring with it much repetition of moral history in Israel,[165] or explaining the slow but certain development of the new order among men by the use of familiar processes or occupations,[166] is represented as setting forth fundamental principles of a practical moral community of men who heed.

It is not alone in parables that this evangelist teaches his readers what he understands by the Kingdom of God. At the time of Jesus' public appearance John Baptist was proclaiming to the people the imminence of the new era which they had been earnestly looking for as a relief from their want and distress, as well as a national achievement before all the nations. John was an ascetic type,[167] quite in contrast to Jesus. His message was one of immediate repentance or summary judgment,[168] not one of patient reconstruction of society. Matthew does not represent John as expounding the Kingdom which he announces, for preacher and hearers knew perfectly what its character was to be. Preparation for the enjoyment of this new era was, according to John, "repent," "bring to light the products of repentance" without depending too fully upon Abrahamic descent. The First Evangelist, unlike Luke,[169] gives no detailed instructions to various classes as to their duties in the emergency, but baptizes all who obey his summons, thus doubtless enlisting their cooperation as his disciples and coworkers for immediate reform.

---

[164] 13. 24–30, 47–50; 25. 14–30, 31–46.
[165] 21. 23–46; 22. 1–10. [166] 13. 1–9, 31–32, 33, 44, 45f.
[167] 3. 4; 11. 8, 18. [168] 3. 2, 10, 12. [169] Luke 3. 10–14.

Jesus indicates the contrast between his method and John's[170] acknowledging that John was indeed his precursor, paying a high compliment to him as a hero of reform, yet scarcely admitting that John entered into the program of the Kingdom as Jesus himself set it forth. "He that is less in the Reign of God is greater than he."[171] The violent measures of the "forerunner" were not in any way adopted by the real prophet of the Kingdom, Jesus.[172]

The parable of the leaven, which "a woman hid . . . till . . . all was leavened," in no way corresponds to John's simile of the ax lying ready to fell the unworthy tree, or of the winnowing fan, ready at once to separate the wheat from the chaff. To be sure, Matthew has Jesus use the very words of John in his opening message, "Repent! for the Kingdom of Heaven is near!"[173] but in his further portrayal of Jesus and his teaching of the Kingdom, the First Evangelist indicates surely how wide a difference existed between the two men and their concept of the new order.[174]

Aside from the teaching of the Sermon on the Mount, which cannot here be rehearsed, the choice of the teaching material in chapters 18 and 15 is sufficiently convincing of Matthew's own conception of a Kingdom that does not come by catastrophe, as many of his fellow Israelites believed, but, rather, of a new era inaugurated within the existing society of Jewish Christianity, in which mutual love between fellow members of the new community was war-

[170] Matt. 11. 11ff. [171] 11. 11b.

[172] In the fifties, it appears from Acts 18. 24—19. 7, the John Baptist movement was parallel to but apart from the Christian "Way."

[173] 3. 2, compare 4. 17.

[174] See above, pp. 118f., summary on the Sermon on the Mount.

ranted and inspired by the nature and example of the Father of them all.[175]

What, then, of the aspect of the Kingdom generally referred to as the apocalyptic?

Matt. 8. 12 offers a unique use of the term "kingdom," which is clearly eschatological. Its context is the statement of Jesus concerning the centurion, whose faith surpassed that of Israelites. Said Jesus:

> "Many shall come from east and west and they shall recline with Abraham and Isaac and Jacob in the Kingdom of the heavens, but the sons of the Kingdom shall be cast forth into the outer darkness, and there shall be weeping and the gnashing of the teeth."[176]

In one other place in the Gospel the term "sons of the Kingdom,"[177] in explanation of "the good seed" among which the tares (darnel) grew up, is used in quite another sense, if 8. 12 is to be interpreted in an eschatological sense. For these "sons of the Kingdom" in chapter 13 are clearly men who live in an earthly environment. The parable of the Tares, however, possesses very apparent eschatological elements at its close.

In 21. 43 Jesus threatens the Israelites who are described in the preceding parable of the Wicked Husbandmen with a withdrawal from them of the Kingdom of Heaven, that it may be given to a nation which brings forth the fruits of the Kingdom.[178] Here the Kingdom can hardly be the future, apoca-

---

[175] 18. 21f.; 15. 7–9, 19f.; compare 5. 43–48; 12. 46–50.

[176] This evangelist in several places favors a movement of the nations of the earth toward Judaism or Jewish-Christianity. This is hardly the type of universalism held by Paul and later Christians.

[177] 13. 38. [178] See 21. 33–43.

lyptic day of blessing, but something that can be transferred from one to another of competing peoples.

In Matt. 3. 2, John Baptist, as suggested above, had an immediate, and probably eschatological type of Kingdom in mind. But Jesus put a different content into the same words, quoted by the evangelist, as to the nearness of the new order.[179]

There is doubtless a reference to later aspects of the Kingdom in 7. 21, "Not every one who says to me, Lord, Lord, shall enter into the Kingdom of Heaven," since the context has certain future judgments in view. The sequel, "but he who does the will of my Father in heaven," shall enter in, reminds one of the principle enunciated by Mark,[180] and repeated by Matthew.[181] An ethical relationship involves "becoming a son of the Father,"[182] the evangelist holds, and he is so certain that only he who endures "to the end" shall find full self-realization that he presents this saying of the Master twice.[183]

In the parables of chapter 13 are found such statements as 13. 41–43, the foregoing context of which[184] has been cited. The words: "The Son of man shall send forth his angels and they shall gather up out of his Kingdom all the stumbling blocks and those who work iniquity," imply that during a process of development there have arisen within the Kingdom unworthy men. The picture

---

[179] There is manuscript authority for a different reading here: "Nigh is the Kingdom of Heaven," omitting "Repent . . . for" (Matt. 4. 17).

[180] Mark 3. 34f., see p. 72 above. [181] Matt. 12. 46–50.

[182] Matt. 5. 45. [183] 10. 22b; 24. 13.

[184] 13. 38.

is that of a future aspect of the development of the new order, perhaps so extreme a point in its development that the unworthy must be "gathered out" in the interest of the Kingdom itself. The language here and in other parts of the first Gospel is traceable to other Jewish writings somewhat contemporary with the early church, which, as the earlier of Paul's letters testify, thought of an impending catastrophic end of the present order. This expectation was not fulfilled. Later New Testament works put less emphasis upon this note.

Of the remaining important examples of the use of apocalyptic language in the First Evangelist's portrayal of the Kingdom should be noted 16. 28, which is a vivid statement on the lips of Jesus that his hearers' generation should not all pass away before the coming of the Son of man "in his Kingdom"; 20. 21, the request of the mother of Zebedee's sons that they might occupy places of distinction in the Kingdom, evidently having a future kingdom of glory and power in mind; 25. 1ff., which picturesquely figures the sudden coming of the Son of man as a bridegroom, for whom await ten maidens. The coming is at length so sudden that the unprepared are shut out of the festivities. 25. 31 continues the discourse upon the coming of the Son of man, this time prepared to judge, that is, separate the unworthy, the unprepared, those who have not in the past offered their fellows such sympathetic service as they should from those who had served, who were worthy, prepared.

Finally there is the statement upon Jesus' lips:[185]

"I declare to you that from now on I shall

[185] 26. 29.

not drink of this fruit of the vine until that day when I drink it new with you in the Kingdom of my Father."

This statement reflects the view that a day of rejoicing, as well as a day of judgment is coming. This picture is that of the triumphant, matured, completed community of sons of the Father. The Kingdom here meant is the same that is proclaimed by Jesus as he addresses his hearers, but at a future stage.

The evidence adduced from the first Gospel shows that in the evangelist's view the Kingdom was one, beginning like a very minute and apparently weak plant, but proceeding onward to full maturity. It must be, in its earlier and middle stages, a part of human life, modifying human life as leaven modifies and transforms the mass. During its human history many unworthy and unkingdom-like men will be drawn into its fellowship or will seek its shelter. An altered behavior alone will not constitute a son of the Father, whose the Kingdom is, and one who resists the inner transformation will be his own judge, for he cannot abide in the future day of triumph and maturity for this movement of inner purity and power.

The life that men live is the field of the real Kingdom. Men who become "sons of the Father" will still pursue their daily vocations, will mingle with their friends in social converse, will enter into contracts, will engage in financial operations. But the spirit and motive with which they do all these things will correspond to the life within, which is the developing nature of their Father. Sympathetic service will be spontaneous, philanthropy and prayer will evidence their real relation to God and to men, but will not of themselves constitute that relation. The "Kingdom of Heaven," paradoxically enough, is a rational, practical, constructive moral program engaged in by men who do the known will of their Father in heaven.

Assignments for Class Reports

1. Show that Matthew is not self-contradictory in his statements about the Kingdom of Heaven.
2. Paraphrase Matt. 25. 31–46 to show its social meaning.
3. Make a list of the parables of the Kingdom found only in Matthew. Does this group of parables contain any unique teaching as to the Kingdom?
4. From what Jewish works do the statements about the appearance of the Son of man at a future time seem to be drawn?

CHAPTER IV

THE ETHICS OF THE GOSPEL ACCORDING TO LUKE

PROPORTION OF DISCOURSE OF JESUS IN LUKE; THIS EVANGELIST'S UNIQUE CONTRIBUTION OF ETHICAL TEACHING

THE third Gospel is longer than the first, containing about 21,000 (Greek) words. Altogether there are 9,239 words placed by Luke upon Jesus' lips and 5,298 of these words occur within the so-called "long insertion" of 9. 51–18. 14. Within these nine chapters are found a large number of parables, many of which are without parallel.

Compared with Mark and Matthew, Luke stands highest in narrative material, and is second only to Matthew in discourse. Chapter 12 is richest in Jesus' teaching, containing some 968 words. All chapters excepting 1 and 3 have some of his words, chapter 2 having fifteen.

The Third Evangelist offers much teaching that has no parallel in the other synoptics, a fact explained, no doubt, by the theory that Luke had access to sources not open to the other Gospel writers. The narrative of this Gospel follows quite closely the order of Mark, yet in his Gospel as a whole Luke has often struck out upon paths of his own and he has withal breathed a spirit into his work which differentiates the third Gospel from all the others.

ACCORDING TO LUKE

THE parables of Luke are often noted for their large number and their intense human interest. Among those peculiar to the third Gospel there are some so familiar that many of their phrases have become proverbial. Interest in social problems, in class distinctions, in the proper use of property, in the nature of prayer to God, in the duty and the rights of the humble as well as of the high, is well sustained by Luke in these short stories of Jesus.

A strange parable, that of 16. 1–13, wherein Jesus' hearers are urged to "make friends out of the unrighteous mammon," yet the tale in no wise contradicts the teaching of the story of the Rich Farmer who confused the scale of values.[1] Luke understood Jesus to teach that wealth as such has its uses.

But material goods are not worthy of chief emphasis, as another parable,[2] selected from his own sources, points out. In this story, a man who had all that heart could wish in this life is shown, by the lifting of the curtain drawn over the future, to be in desperate want. His goods were not enduring. But a good man, though poor, who had begged in vain at the rich man's door, appears in contrast to his one time social superior to be enjoying "Abraham's bosom." The rich man is scored, not for his wealth as such, for Abraham himself was one of the richest men in the Old Testament, but rather for his failure to "make a friend" rather than an enemy out of the wealth entrusted to him.

The so-called "parable of the pounds"[3] stresses the point that good use is to be made of any goods entrusted to one.

---

[1] 12. 16–21. [2] 16. 19–31. [3] 19. 11–27.

Any catalog of the Lukan material that concerns the conservation of wealth must include the parables of the One Lost Sheep,[4] the Small Coin that Was Lost,[5] and the Unproductive Tree which was worth much patient toil even in the hope that its value would repay.[6] The whole story involved in the last reference appears to contrast with the patient gardener the spirit of summary judgment, as found in the words of the ardent Baptist: "Every tree that does not produce good fruit shall be felled and burned."

Doubtless the most remarkable parables in Luke deal with personal relations within the community. The Merciful Samaritan[7] indicts forever the complacent selfishness of the socially and ecclesiastically exalted.

Many of the conventional relations in which men of his time found themselves are used by Jesus in these parables of Luke to teach the ideal relations between men and between men and the Father in the new ethical community. A Persistent Seeker and his Selfish Neighbor at Night[8] offer a contrast to the Father who is ready to grant good things to sincere seekers.[9] The evangelist selects another parable to enforce this teaching in 18. 1–8. The judge who vindicated a persistent client only to be rid of him is in sharp contrast to the Father who will "avenge his elect speedily."

Immediately follows[10] a unique story of two men who offered prayer to God in quite different atti-

---

[4] 15. 1–7. [5] 15. 8–10.
[6] Luke 13. 6–9. See below, Luke and the Synoptics in their Attitude Toward Property for further consideration of this data.
[7] 10. 29–37. [8] 11. 5–8.
[9] 11. 9–13. [10] 18. 9–14.

tudes. The spirit within a man counts more than his social position. Luke leaves no doubt that this story was directed at "certain people who were persuaded in themselves that they were about right and who counted all others out."

Besides the foregoing parables there are eight or nine instances of more or less formal address by Jesus in the third Gospel which offer distinct ethical contributions. Some of these find exposition in later sections.

Some of these addresses bear the form of parables, as the story of the Two Debtors, which formed the ground of a reproof to a Pharisee, Simon by name, who had treated Jesus none too courteously yet criticized all too gratuitously his gracious treatment of an ostracized woman.[11] Another much-needed lesson in etiquette was applied to both guests and host, when[12] the Master noted the self-seeking that characterized the social behavior of his contemporaries.

Luke describes in his own terms the repudiation of Jesus as a social prophet by his townspeople[13] and in two other passages[14] describes two types of servant and their appropriate reward, perhaps with the high example of Jesus himself in mind.

The address to the Seventy, whom Jesus sent out "into every city and place to which he himself intended to come"[15] may be supplemented by recalling Jesus' own call to repentance,[16] his proposal of strict conditions of discipleship[17] and possibly his declaration to the Pharisees of 17. 20–21:

[11] 7. 40–50. [12] 14. 7–14. [13] 4. 16–30.
[14] 12. 42–48; 17. 7–10. [15] 10. 1–16.
[16] 13. 1–9. [17] 14. 28–35.

"The Kingdom of God does not come after the fashion of sense perception, nor shall people say, Look here, or there! For in fact the Kingdom of God is within you."

Assignments for Class Reports

1. Compare the words of Jesus in the Nazareth synagogue with the passage in Isaiah 61. 1 and note (*a*) the accuracy of the quotation, and (*b*) whether the prophet had somewhat the same meaning in his words as here represented by Luke.
2. What distinction is made between the "disciples" and "apostles" of Luke 6. 13? Do you understand that at this time many people were seriously attempting to follow Jesus? If so, for what reason?
3. Do you identify Levi of Luke 5. 29 with Matt. of 6. 15? If so, upon what evidence?
4. Upon precisely what grounds do you suppose the fellow townsmen of Jesus sought to assault him? (4. 28–29.)
5. Find any passages in Mark which are parallel to Luke 4. 41. Describe in your own words what really happened.

The Sermon on the Plain: Jesus' Law of Social Amity, According to Luke

The first discourse in Luke is found in chapter 6. Following the gospel of the infancy and youth of Jesus,[18] appear John Baptist's call to repentance,[19] the baptism of Jesus,[20] his genealogy,[21] his retirement,[22] in which Satan "completed every temptation," after which the public teaching of the Lord is begun.[23]

[18] Luke, chapters 1 and 2. [19] 3. 2–20.
[20] 3. 21f. [21] 3. 23–38. [22] 4. 1–13. [23] 4. 14ff.

His own townspeople reject their prophet,[24] but others[25] are astonished at his authoritative manner of teaching, and his fame spreads widely.

Although Jesus begins his public ministry in the synagogue,[26] it appears that the multitude of hearers soon compel him to teach out of doors,[27] or in any house where he happens to be.[28]

Healings accompany the teaching in the synagogue and by the seaside,[29] and at the point where Luke places this discourse Jesus has excited the hostile interest of Pharisees and doctors from Jerusalem[30] as well as that of his fellow townsmen.

In the Sermon on the Plain the Third Evangelist details the instruction of his disciples when Jesus separates from their number twelve "apostles." It is clear that the company was by no means small[31] and that much interest in the curing power of the Teacher was continually adding to the number of followers.

The presence of a large number of needy people, socially submerged, poor, hungry, in tears, hated of their fellows,[32] seems to turn the Teacher's mind toward the problem of the social order, split up into layers distinct from one another, with the lines of cleavage probably becoming more rather than less distinct.

It forms an opportune occasion for a pronouncement upon the cure of a distressing situation and upon the constructive program in which these "disciples" must engage in order to bring about their social, moral, and spiritual redemption.

[24] 4. 28ff. [25] 4. 32, 37. [26] 4. 44.
[27] 5. 16ff. [28] For example, 5. 29.
[29] 4. 33ff., 38f., 40ff.; 5. 12ff., 18ff.; 6. 6ff., 19.
[30] 5. 17ff. [31] 6. 17. [32] 6. 20–22.

The address may be paraphrased thus:

My disciples, many of you find that life brings you poverty with its accompanying hunger and distress, moreover, much sorrow fills your days and men look down upon you. Yet all this does not disqualify you for the finer joys that come to men engaged in high moral endeavor. History records that men of the past who are believed to be among the most favored of God had a similar lot. On the other hand, you rich, you joyful, you satisfied and you who are applauded, are not by these tokens alone to be congratulated. For these may presage loss and disaster.

I have this word to say, with emphasis: Abandon the superficial rule of the day, and serve even those who are against you, cultivate a brotherly attitude toward even your adversaries, do good instead of evil in every respect, taking as the measure of your conduct the rule, "As you would that men should do to you, do likewise unto them."

While such a policy may to some appear futile, I assure you it is the very way in which the Father deals with his creatures. All men are not thankful to him, yet he brings the common blessings upon the ungodly as upon the good. In loving even your enemies you establish your own sonship with the Father.

Set a positive example that seems to you good, without waiting to see what your advantages will be. Do not be censorious, mean, niggardly. For it is a common rule that like begets like in this world. And your example may make others generous and brotherly.[33]

This law of social amity Jesus enforced with many illustrations. It takes a man who has eyes to guide the blind. It needs a teacher who knows his subject to instruct his pupil. One ought not try to take a speck from his neighbor's eye until one's own eye is clear. Thus it is in nature, a good tree is needed to produce perfect fruit, and the appropriate fruit comes only from the tree fitted by nature to bear it. Men identify the tree by its fruit. It takes a good man to do good deeds. The proverb has it, "Out of the fullness of the heart one's mouth speaks."

"My disciples," said the Teacher in effect, "are called upon to lead and not to follow. They are the chosen men of insight, who shall show men that they are indeed sons of the Most High, and as such, shall show the community that the Father's way of doing things is productive of the greatest good."

"I shall be most disappointed with that man who hears me, who sees clearly what I mean and yet does not follow my teaching. He is like a senseless builder who trusts a costly edifice to an insecure foundation."[34]

It is clear to the reader that Luke understands these words of Jesus as formal instruction addressed to his disciples. The subject is "The Kingdom of God," as verse 29 indicates. "You poor, you are to be congratulated, for the Kingdom of God is yours."

---

[33] Luke 6. 20–38. [34] Luke 6. 39–49.

The words of John Baptist[35] bring to remembrance the vivid portrayal of God's coming, as the great prophet of the Return had foretold,[36] and Jesus' opening address in the synagogue at Nazareth[37] was accompanied by an appeal to ancient words,[38] which the speaker declared were fulfilled in himself. These passages from Jewish Scriptures promise a better moral and social order in which the people of God will live. Such a golden day to come was the substance of many a prophet's vision. Jesus' message, as Luke understands it, carried the conviction to his intimate hearers that the new order was imminent. This new order was the Reign of God.

Even more pointedly than Matthew, Luke identifies the classes who shall be eligible for membership in the new order. Not the most prominent, but the most needy are those to whom the call comes.

While the meaning of this term, "Kingdom of God," for the Third Evangelist must await more thorough examination of his Gospel, it is clear thus far that it concerns a program for betterment of human living conditions and that it is a program that involves the activity of chosen men in the moral sphere. All the conditions set forth in the Sermon on the Plain are conditions of human life.

This Sermon is much shorter than the Sermon on the Mount. While much material is parallel, its arrangement in each case is individually determined. Luke will offer more parables as vehicles of Jesus' teaching of the Kingdom. Thus he does not need to

---

[35] Luke 3. 4ff.
[36] Isa. 40. 3ff.
[37] Luke 4. 16ff.
[38] Isa. 61. 1ff.

carry his formal Sermon to such a length as did the First Evangelist.

The outstanding teaching of the pericope is that men, Jesus' disciples, are to become conspicuous leaders in a program that involves unselfish and often unrewarded service of others; that this is the Master's and the Father's attitude toward all, hence the disciple will imitate the highest example offered to men. Such an example of disinterested service will at length become infectious, and to the extent to which this becomes true, a high degree of social amity will result.

Assignments for Class Reports

1. What classes in Jewish society appear in the first six chapters of Luke?
2. Compare the number of topics treated in Luke's Sermon with the number of topics in Matthew's Sermon.
3. What is the theme of Luke 6. 20–49?
4. What emphasis upon "reward" do you find in Luke's Sermon?
5. How is the selection of the Twelve placed respectively by Matthew and Luke?
6. What different effect, if any, does Luke obtain from the placing of his words about fasting (5. 33ff.) and the Sabbath (6. 1ff.) as compared with Matthew's teaching on these points?

Ethics and Conventionality: Jesus' Treatment of the Socially Unfit

Among the Jewish people class distinctions were strictly drawn. The Pharisee dwelt upon the difference between himself and "other men," especially the publican who for the moment came within his vision,[39] social outcasts did favors for those within their own circle,[40] the priest and the Levite hesitated to touch a common man even to aid him in distress,[41] guests at a feast were inclined to choose for themselves places of honor, although the arrival of one in a more favored class might bring humiliation,[42] the rich were particularly apt to be self-centered,[43] and in general, conditions as Jesus observed them led him to urge tolerance and catholicity, even affection and interest in and for men of all classes.[44]

In Palestine there appeared to be in many minds an implicit assumption that God himself had established the different classes among men to correspond with his love and care for them. The third Gospel notably devotes attention to the various classes to whom Jesus rendered service, thus offering ground for supposing that the Teacher considered such an assumption unethical.

In the synoptics generally the deliberate breaking of social barriers by Jesus[45] was in the eyes of the religious leaders an offensive action, but Luke understands that Jesus' persistence in this practice was an object lesson to reinforce his teaching that real values in men are not determined by outward marks, such as wealth, social position, or office. The Third Evangelist presents in a large number of passages[46] his attitude toward the Jewish social observances as modified or criticized by Jesus.

[39] Luke 18. 9–14. [40] 6. 34f. [41] 10. 29–37. [42] 14. 7–14.
[43] 14. 13–21; 16. 14, 19–31. [44] 13. 1–9; 9. 51–56; 7. 36–50.
[45] For example, Matt. 9. 10ff.; Mark 2. 15ff.; 7. 26.
[46] Characteristic portions are Luke 6. 34f.; 7. 36–50; 9. 51–56; 10. 29–37; 12. 13–21; 13. 1–5; 14. 7–14; 16. 14f., 19–31; 18. 9–14; 19. 1–10. There is no doubt that the conventional social life of the Jewish people is correctly reflected in these passages.

Says Jesus, in substance, a man has, in his own right, distinct possibilities of moral development. Any convention or institution that tends to hinder a man's moral development, when measured beside the man, must yield. When it amounts to public neglect of men, the convention that thus dictates is itself immoral.[47]

There is perhaps nothing more human than to reverence an ancient institution, particularly if it possesses a religious sanction. The Sabbath among the Jewish people was such an institution. Jesus found men surrounding the Sabbath with restrictions that seemed to him irrational. The disciples were challenged for rubbing grains of wheat in their hands on that day,[48] but Jesus returned answer that King David had the insight even to eat bread that was hallowed, thus setting human need above ceremonial ritual. Again the Master made reply to his critics[49] that a poor woman, a daughter of Abraham, was rightfully restored to health on the Sabbath.[50]

Conventions, in any society, tend to become tyrannical. Frequently they lag behind moral discovery and fail to keep pace with developing social needs. When this is the case, says Jesus, let the conventional give place to that which best serves the highest personal values, such as inner purity, manliness, love for fellow men, honor, character itself.

Distinctions between classes were found by the

---

[47] See particularly Luke 13. 10–17 and 14. 1–6.
[48] Luke 6. 2. [49] Luke 13. 16.
[50] Compare Luke 11. 31b, 32 in the light of Professor Bacon's note on the translation of "greater than," Journal of Religion, vol. iv, p. 259f., 1924.

evangelist to be barriers between him who would serve and those who most needed services. Very instructive is the story in Luke 7. 36–50, in which figured a Pharisee as host, Jesus as guest, and a woman from an ostracized class, who came in to anoint the Master with tears and perfume. In other Gospels complaint is made in similar cases as to the waste of the perfume. Here it is strictly a social contact that is questioned. The Pharisee argues that Jesus did not divine her character, else he would not have allowed her to touch him.[51] But the sequel shows that Jesus clearly knew her character and her need. Furthermore, he satisfied that need. Then he related a story to his host, Simon, carrying the plain yet effective lesson that this person, despised by the Pharisee class, was actually in a situation to love him more than those who felt less need.

With Jesus, social service was far more than a word. The desire to serve led him to encounter the strongest social taboos and to break them when the alleviation of need was possible.

Luke furnishes his reader with a fairly detailed account of the field of service as Jesus understood it; or, in modern terms, it may be said that Luke defined the ethics of social service by the use of a variety of examples of Jesus' teaching and practice.

The Reign of God as a moral program had its field in the social life of the people of his day, Luke seems to say. The Master feasted alike with Pharisees and publicans, with those who believed themselves models of "righteousness" and with those who knew themselves to be sinners and despised.

[51] 7. 39.

In fact, to these latter Jesus promised the greater felicity.[52] The sick needed the physician, one's neighbor is that one who is in need, whatever his status. Social service would tend to obliterate artificial barriers that hindered its beneficent spread.

Assignments for Class Reports

1. After a study of Luke 4. 18ff.; 5. 12ff.; 5. 27–29; 7. 22; 11. 38ff. and similar passages, indicate the character of the class barriers in Jesus' way. Give references for any additional portions studied.
2. In what ways does Luke teach that formalism may become a substitute for moral practice?
3. Define conventionality and discuss the competition between conventionality and ethics in terms of present-day life. Which of the two should have the greater authority? Which probably has the greater force in your community?
4. Identify any conventional practices that now prevail, yet which are not abreast of recognized social need.
5. In what way can you defend the thesis that morality is the same for all classes of people? To what degree can the existence of class distinctions be justified?
6. What passages in Luke may be said to deal with etiquette? To what extent does etiquette lie in the field of ethics?

The Ethics of Propaganda

Luke makes it plain to his reader that Jesus desired to spread his teaching at least among his fellow countrymen, for this evangelist has an account of the sending of the Twelve upon a mission,[53] and in addition narrates[54] that the Lord "appointed

[52] 6. 22. [53] Chapter 9. [54] Chapter 10.

seventy others," with a view to sending them ahead of him. Presumably all this activity was confined to Jewish people and Jewish territory.[55]

Luke agrees with the other synoptic Gospel writers that Jesus made effort to propagate his message widely during his lifetime, and that he made provision for the spread of the "good news" after his demise. Even in the first Gospel occur words that are sometimes interpreted to sanction an unrestricted appeal to all nations to become Jesus' disciples, without reference to Judaism,[56] although the sequel, as far as the book of Acts records, favors the view that the disciples at first put a more restricted interpretation upon the Great Commission of Matt. 28. 19, Luke 24. 47, and Acts 1. 8. Certain it is that the religious teachers of Judaism made strenuous efforts to propagate their views and win proselytes, as Jesus himself declares,[57] although without approval of the views thus propagated. Paul of Tarsus, a Pharisee of the second or third generation, well illustrates the missionary zeal of those who held the Jewish Torah to contain the supreme revelation of God to men.

All the synoptic evangelists agree that Jesus sought to spread the "good news" of the imminent Reign of God most widely. Mark[58] says that Jesus appointed the Twelve "that he might send them forth to herald the good news"; Matthew[59] says he sent the Twelve "to the lost sheep of the house of Israel" while upon their Galilæan mission, but after Jesus' resurrection[60] "all the nations" are included

[55] Luke 9. 6, "through the villages,"; 10. 1, "every place into which he himself was about to come."
[56] Matt. 28. 19. [57] Matt. 23. 15.
[58] 3. 14. [59] 10. 6. [60] Matt. 28. 19.

in their mission. Luke imposes no territorial restrictions upon the apostles of the Galilæan period, and after the resurrection thinks of Jesus as sending his followers to "all the nations," although the beginning should be at Jerusalem. The Third Evangelist, indeed, seems to hold that all this propaganda had scriptural sanction, for in 24. 44ff. he represents the Master as saying:

> "These are my words which I spoke to you while I was still with you, namely, that all things which are written in the law of Moses and in the prophets and in the psalms concerning me must be fulfilled. Then he opened their mind to the understanding of the Scriptures, and he said to them: Thus it is written . . . that repentance and remission of sin should be preached in his name unto all the nations, beginning from Jerusalem."

Thus while all the synoptics agree in the view that Jesus was interested in spreading the "good news," Luke, with his mission of the Seventy, his appeal to scriptural sanction for the continued propaganda after the death of the Master and his many expressions indicating the conviction of Jesus that he was directed by the Father to proclaim widely his message of the coming new order of things,[61] a task and responsibility which he shared with his disciples, emphasizes more than the others the interest of Jesus in reaching the many with his message.

The book of Acts, written by the Third Evangelist, contains abundant evidence that the disciples

[61] 4. 18–21; 4. 43; 5. 32; 7. 22f.; 8. 1; 9. 1ff.; 10. 2; 19. 47f.; 21. 37f.; 22. 35–38.

carried out a vigorous program of preaching and making converts to "the Way," as Jesus' program was called in those days. Whether Luke wrote into his Gospel the impression of serious campaigning for Jesus' ideal which he saw during his companionship with Paul may remain an open question. It is certain, at all events, that this evangelist heartily endorsed such a program and that he believed it to be entirely within the plan of the Master.

The reader of the third Gospel cannot fail to note that Jesus and his disciples set out with the intention of bringing men into their following, in response to no express invitation on the part of those sought but, rather, in response to the mute appeal which their need offered. Jesus likened the people of Galilee to "sheep unshepherded" and again to a harvest field wasted for lack of harvesters.[62]

The ethical significance of this is obvious. Whether Jesus himself made missionary journeys outside of Israel or not, his words were pregnant with missionary meaning. It may even be admitted that Jesus did not expressly teach his disciples that "all nations" should be directly invited to share their fellowship, in fact, such an admission may be demanded by the very limitations under which the work of Jesus was carried on. But it cannot be doubted that soon after the death of Jesus the Reign of God appeared to the understanding of his most advanced disciples as a program that involved all men. The monotheism of Judaism logically demanded a Fatherhood of God, the only living God, which in turn demanded a brotherhood of men. The Reign of God could be complete

[62] Luke 10. 2.

only when all men were included under its sway. Thus Jesus' teaching, as it ripened in the thought of the disciples, called for the inclusion of all nations within its meaning, as the distinct teaching of the Kingdom had clearly demanded the inclusion of all moral aspects of human living under its sway.

Assignments for Class Reports

1. Compare the reported words of Jesus in Luke 24. 45–49 with those in Acts 1. 8 and in Matt. 28. 19a. Which passage most implicitly directs the disciples to present Jesus' program without respect to the demands of Judaism? Does either passage seem more original than others?
2. Find in the book of Acts the place which describes the first instance of direct evangelizing of Greek people. What is the date of this attempt?
3. Of the two Gospels, Matthew and Luke, which offers the greater evidence of the universal character of Jesus' mission? Present the evidence in compact form.
4. In what way can you justify the uninvited propagation of such a program as that of Jesus' Reign of God?
5. Can it be shown that the present-day "social gospel" is justified in its demand that all business relations be submitted to the law of the Kingdom as Jesus taught it?

The Ethics of Material Possessions: Luke and the Other Synoptic Writers

The synoptic Gospels generally assume that men who have submitted themselves to the Reign of God shall still engage in business, own property, and doubtless collect rental, permit interest to accrue and maintain their property in good condition. While one man is called upon to renounce all his wealth,[63] another[64] may be received with no demand that he part with his goods. It is said of one of the Twelve, Levi,[65] doubtless with approval, that he "forsook everything" to follow Jesus. In the context Levi spends a noticeable amount of money to "make a great feast in his house" in honor of Jesus. Luke supports the view that men within the Kingdom were still to own property, just as Mark and Matthew hold that the field of the Kingdom is the world of persons in their economic, industrial, and domestic surroundings.[66] For Jesus addressed those who manifestly are within the Reign of God, saying, "Lend, never despairing"[67] and "give."[68] Thus the evangelist assumes that these disciples are to own something which they can lend or give. True, the measure of property owned may not be large, in the thought of the evangelist, for he reminds his readers that upon sending his seventy missioners forth Jesus said to them:

> "Do not carry a purse, or an alms-bag [wallet], or shoes; and do not salute anyone along the way. Remain in the same house, eating and drinking what they have. For worthy the laborer of his pay. Do not move from house to house."[69]

As in the second and first Gospels, the disciple is warned against making property as such the chief object of interest. His followers are to "seek the Kingdom"[70] which, indeed, the Father will make readily available,[71] and with it all needed material things. "Your Father knows that you have need

[63] Luke 18. 22. [64] 19. 9. [65] Luke 5. 28.
[66] See Luke 4. 18; 10. 9; 17. 21 et al. [67] Luke 6. 35.
[68] 6. 38. [69] Luke 10. 4–7. [70] Luke 12. 31. [71] 12. 32.

of these things."[72] The moral lies close at hand,[73] that the chief interests of a man will be directed intensely in the direction of his most highly prized possessions. So it may be necessary or advisable to sell what one has and use the proceeds in giving alms, for the purse that does not grow old and the values which may neither be defaced or stolen are, after all, most appropriate for the disciple.[74] Yet normally Jesus seems, in the estimation of the Third Evangelist, to teach that property should rightly remain in the control of the men of the Kingdom, and that such property should be made productive.

For in the short stories or parables so often used in his teaching in the third Gospel Jesus more than implies the desirability of seeing property productive rather than idle. The man who owned a fig tree that did not bear[75] would summarily replace it, but his gardener sought time and opportunity to make it fruitful. The man who had a hundred sheep went after the one that had strayed, illustrating primarily[76] the one repentant sinner, contrasted with the many who need not to repent, nevertheless citing the action of the shepherd as natural and commendable. Otherwise the parable would fail of its purpose. The rich man of Luke 16. 19ff. merits condemnation not so much for being rich as for his personal attitude toward the needy brother at his gate. For in the sequel is found a rich man on each side of the abyss, Dives and Abraham.

Upon any fair interpretation of the parable of

[72] 12. 30. [73] 12. 34. [74] Luke 12. 33.
[75] 13. 6ff. [76] 15. 7.

the Wasteful Steward[77] the evangelist represents Jesus as commending a proper care for property, whether one's own or another's, and even as advising a diplomatic use of wealth. But this attitude of Jesus is also clearly defended on the part of Luke only as it is modified by the caution that such property holds a subordinate place in the life of a man of the Kingdom. The ultimate teaching of Luke here should be compared with that of Matthew in the Sermon on the Mount: "You cannot serve God and mammon."

Jesus himself did not lead an abstemious life. Charges were brought against him,[78] at least concerning his disciples, involving the generous use of food: "The disciples of John fast often and offer supplication, just as the disciples of the Pharisees do, but yours are eating and drinking."[79]

Luke does not indicate in any way that the Jewish leaders or Jesus condemned the centurion of 7.2–10 for his possession of such wealth that he could become a benefactor of the Jewish community in building them a synagogue. Jesus clearly commends the man for an inner quality not found in some Jewish people. "Not even in Israel did I find such faith!"[80] True, this centurion was not of Jesus' immediate following, but he was a beneficiary of the Master and the latter is reported to have commended a "personal value" found in him. The reader would, indeed, feel a distinct sense of incongruity if there had been inserted in this story of the centurion any condemnation of wealth.

During the mission journeys upon which Jesus

---

[77] Luke 16. 1–8.
[78] 5. 33ff.
[79] See also Luke 7. 33f.
[80] 7. 9b.

sent his disciples they were to dispense with superfluous goods[81] and depend upon the bounty of the people to whom they preached. But at the close of Jesus' ministry he distinctly told his followers[82] that these conditions were to change and that they must go out with equipment. The sequel indicates that the disciples interpreted these words conservatively, for Paul insisted upon working for his own living while preaching the Kingdom, and perhaps no disciple in the apostolic period acquired much of this world's goods. But it is not apparent that any of them understood that Jesus condemned property as such. Such a story as that of Ananias and Sapphira in Acts 5, however, teaches that the apostles had a lively sense of values in the use of money or other property. For Ananias was rebuked not so much for holding back a part of the price as for misrepresenting the transaction.

Neither did Jesus, according to the Third Evangelist, condemn the scrupulous tithing of income from the garden, a practice carried on by the most punctilious sect, the Pharisees. There is nothing wrong in such minute estimates of offering to God, to be sure, for this tithing is not to be left undone. Yet if such practice be substituted for the practice of justice and for the genuine love of God, it is immoral. In Luke 11. 42–44 the evangelist teaches his reader that personal relations, especially those involving social-ethical practices, are first in order of importance.

A most important deliverance of Jesus reported by Luke[83] gives with great clearness the evangelist's

---

[81] 9. 3ff.; 10. 7. [82] 22. 35f. [83] 12. 13ff.

understanding of the Master's mind on the property question. A listener attempts to win the influence of the Teacher in his dispute with other heirs as to a certain inheritance. Jesus refuses to become a party to his dispute, but interests himself in the higher values involved. "See that you keep yourself on guard against all forms of covetousness; for it is not upon the abundance of possessions that a man's life is based." The evangelist further illustrates the remark by a parable having to do with a farmer who considered that a prosperous year with its abundant crops assured him of all that a hungry soul desired. But the soul appears to be dependent upon other than material nourishment.

The foregoing occasion was used also for admonition of the disciples themselves.[84] "The life is more than nourishment and the body itself more than its clothing. . . . Do not put too much emphasis upon the externals, for the Father will surely provide needful things." The saying found in 12.32 does not seem any too well fitted to its context, but adds to the entire passage a note of beautiful assurance of the Father's intention to bestow upon the disciples of Jesus the *summum bonum*, the benefits of the new order itself, and not merely supply bodily needs.

This survey of the material in the third Gospel that deals with property or material values as such results in a few definite conclusions:

Jesus teaches that the new order concerns itself with social conditions. Men who qualify as citizens of the Kingdom are still citizens of some community on earth.

[84] 12. 22ff.

Material goods are appropriate possessions of citizens of the Kingdom.

Not the amount of material wealth, but its use, counts in its real value to the citizen of the Kingdom; for character, and not wealth, constitutes a man's life.

Moral values inhere in personality, not in wealth as such.

Assignments for Class Reports

1. Show whether the development of a Christian order is compatible with the continuance of modern industrial enterprises. Collect evidence from Luke and other Synoptics to confirm or deny the judgment that to conduct business upon a strictly profit-making basis collides with Jesus' teaching.
2. Illustrate the statement that wealth *per se* cannot have moral value. What truth is found in the expression "tainted money"?
3. To what extent has Christianity actually insisted upon poverty as a basis for membership in the Kingdom of God?
4. Show whether business institutions, for example, banks, factories, transportation systems, and insurance companies, are appropriate in a modern Christian moral order.
5. Gather all the evidence to be found in Luke to support the statement that personal values (that is, nonmaterial values) are supreme.

The Ethics of the Family

There is every reason to suppose that Jesus thought of the family as the unit within the moral community which he termed the Reign of God. The story of Jesus' birth, infancy, and youth, preserved by this evangelist in chapters 1 and 2 of his

Gospel reflects his judgment as to the preeminence of the monogamous family in Christian circles. For the family in which Jesus was reared appears to be exemplary in its inner relations. Not only the evangelist but writers of some other New Testament books use the figure of the family to illustrate the most intimate personal relations between men and God, as well as between men.[85]

In search of Jesus' views as to the ethics of the family, however, as in the case of his teaching about property, as to formal religious observance and other matters, the student will fail to find any set discourse or compendium of directions that will entirely satisfy his inquiries. Practically all of Jesus' teaching which the evangelists have recorded as bearing upon this inquiry is found in the form of answers to specific questions asked of the Teacher, or in response to some further inquiry made in private by his disciples. The Third Evangelist has not recorded as much of Jesus' teaching upon the family relations as the First,[86] however, and the most important passage in Luke[87] is unfortunately without a coherent context, hence difficult to articulate with the Master's other teaching upon the theme.

Since Luke offers no related context to his quotation from Jesus, "He who divorces his wife and marries another commits adultery, and he who marries a divorcee commits adultery," the saying should be studied with reference to words of Jesus reported by Mark and Matthew. As noted above[88]

---

[85] See Mark 3. 31ff.; Luke 12. 32; 15. 11–32; John 14. 8ff.; Rom. 8. 14ff.; Eph. 5. 1, and many similar passages.
[86] Pages 141–145 above should be reviewed here.
[87] 16. 18. [88] Page 142f.

the First Evangelist offers a restriction upon the absolute negation of divorce, which appears in neither of the other synoptics. Thus Mark and Luke are likely to be more closely in harmony.

Mark 10. 11f. reads as follows:

> "Whoever divorces his wife and marries another commits adultery against her; and if she divorces her husband and marries another she commits adultery."[89]

Luke and Mark alike consider the case of divorce which involves remarriage in each case making the statement that such remarriage constitutes a breach of the seventh commandment; Luke further affirms the same of the divorcee who remarries; and Mark takes up the possible case under Roman law in which a wife divorces her husband to remarry, affirming that such a case also constitutes adultery. With one voice these two evangelists assert the immoral nature of divorce which has remarriage as its sequel. There is no unambiguous statement to be found in these Gospels dealing with separation of husband and wife without reference to remarriage. But the statements above considered leave no doubt in the reader's mind that in the evangelist's understanding of Jesus' teaching divorce is unkingdomlike and abnormal. In perhaps all cases noted the immorality involved was entirely antecedent to the divorce proceeding itself.

Divorce, however, is but one aspect of family

---

[89] The order in verse 11 makes it possible to translate: "Whoever divorces his wife and marries another commits adultery with the latter," but the use of the same pronoun ("against her," "she," verse 12) makes it probable that by the expression "against her," as above rendered, Mark was thinking of the first wife of the man in question.

ethics. There is nothing in the third Gospel to contradict the view won by study of the first and second Gospels in their view of the Kingdom of God, namely, that the life of men and women in family relationships is in reality the life of men and women who are subject to the Reign of God even while living under wholly human conditions. Whatever is true of the larger moral community is true of the family relationships. Nothing in the gospels points to Jesus' approval of a harsh attitude toward the offender. The Master freely forgave the sins of the paralytic let down by his friends through the roof,[90] and to the "woman who was a sinner"[91] he said: "Your sins are forgiven." No reader can doubt that the "pericope adulterae,"[92] which is clearly synoptic in style, and perhaps Lukan, teaches that Jesus forgave the social offender in the words, "Go your way, from now on, sin no more."

Yet Jesus makes even family relationships subordinate to Kingdom loyalty. Those very strong words in Luke 14. 25f. bear witness to the supreme claim of the latter:

> "If any one comes to me and does not hate his own father and mother and wife and children and brothers and sisters, yes, even his own life, he cannot be my disciple."

These words are doubtless to be interpreted in the light of other words to be found in the same Gospel, as for example, 18. 29:

> "I solemnly assure you that there is no one who has forsaken home or wife or brothers or parents or children for the sake of the Reign of

[90] Luke 5. 20ff. [91] Luke 7. 48. [92] John 7. 53–8. 11.

God who shall not receive many fold in the present and in the future eternal life."

When someone enthusiastically pronounced blessings upon Jesus' own mother for bearing and rearing him, he returned answer:[93] "Nay, rather blessed are those who hear and perform the word of God!"

The Master in no wise depreciates the sanctity of marriage nor belittles the importance of loyal relations within the family. Such loyalties are entirely harmonious with Kingdom loyalty and may coexist. But when the Gospels were written there had occurred many separations from those who would not go with the disciple upon the way of his Lord. Many a man and woman had actually forsaken parents and had broken conjugal relations for the sake of the Reign of God. The strong words of Luke in his report of Jesus' challenge to his disciples may well be both prophecy and history.

Assignments for Class Reports

1. Investigate Jesus' attitude toward women and children as represented by Luke.
2. What details of Jesus' own family relationships can you reconstruct?
3. Study Luke 16. 18; Mark 10. 11f.; Matt. 19. 9; 5. 32 with reference to the question whether the remarriage element alone made the divorce immoral in Jesus' thought.
4. Show what effect upon frequency of divorce the practical application of the principle of reconciliation would have. Consult the section upon Ethics of the Family in the first Gospel, above, and particularly Matt. 5. 23ff. and 18. 15ff.
5. Do Jesus' words in Matt. 19. 8 indicate that the moral

[93] Luke 11. 28.

status of divorce varies with the times? What do the words teach as to evolution in moral thought?

6. Where in the New Testament, outside the Gospels, do you find any reference to the division of families for the sake of the Kingdom of God?

The View of the Third Evangelist Concerning the Reign of God

In this Gospel, as in the other Synoptics, the student looks in vain for a concise exposition of the Reign of God which can be ascribed to Jesus as a formal, definitive statement. On the other hand, one finds many statements and similes that have for their aim the explanation of this new ethical community. Mark puts much stress upon ethical relations between the members of the community, Matthew emphasizes two sides or aspects of the new order, namely, the present and developing stage, then the perfected or eschatological era of its history. Luke, it is true, points out some words of Jesus that have the apocalyptic tone, but on the whole he thinks of the Kingdom as an ethical program that concerns itself with relations within the social order, with removal of conventional barriers between needy persons and their brothers, with the right use of this world's goods and with effective communion between men and God.

With Mark and Matthew, Luke has his version of the synoptic apocalypse, but neither of the successors of Mark has added notably to the ethical contribution of that passage.[94] Thus there exists no need to discuss it further here.

Once Jesus met some people who were strongly

---

[94] See page 64, footnote 131.

of the opinion that the new era was to be ushered in very soon,[95] to whom he addressed the parable of the pounds. Possibly these people were Jesus' own disciples. However that may be, his story must have given the hearers the impression that this teacher did not sympathize with such immediate expectations. There is much business to do in the meantime.

Upon being asked by certain Pharisees, "When will the Kingdom come?"[96] the Master made one of his most direct answers, in the words: "The Reign of God is within you."

Immediately following this answer, says Luke, Jesus turned to his disciples with a remark couched in apocalyptic language:

> "There shall come the time when you shall yearn to see one of the days of the Son of man, and you shall not see one."[97]

Thereupon follow the words that appear to be related to the synoptic apocalypse. The meaning of the expression "one of the days of the Son of man" is scarcely clear enough here to draw from it any specific teaching as to the Kingdom, present or future.

That the Third Evangelist did in a sense ascribe to Jesus the view that the "coming" of the Kingdom would not be delayed many decades is perhaps clear from 9. 26f.:

> "Who-so-ever shall be ashamed of me and my words, of him shall the Son of man be ashamed when he shall come in his glory and in that of the Father and of the holy angels. But I say to you truly there are certain of those standing

[95] Luke 19. 11ff. [96] Luke 17. 20. [97] 17. 22.

> here who shall by no means taste of death until they see the Kingdom of God."

This saying, placed as it is between the confession of Peter at Cæsarea Philippi and the Transfiguration, has a strangely solemn tone. From the context the reader gathers that the evangelist is enforcing the teaching of Jesus that however soon the Kingdom itself may come, the disciple is to espouse loyalty to its program even if that means death of the body.[98]

> "For whosoever wills to save his life shall lose it, and whosoever loses his life for my sake, this man shall save his life."[99]

Jesus spoke similar words to his disciples,[100] in connection with a warning against the Pharisees:

> "I tell you, my friends, do not fear those who kill the body, but who can do nothing further than that. But I will show you whom you should fear. Fear him who has power after he has killed to cast you into Gehenna, yes, I tell you, Fear him."

Luke also puts words on the lips of Jesus that describe his own fate in the language of the apocalyptic writers of his time. Jesus' message to Herod, when warned by his friends among the Pharisees,[101] reads:

> "Lo, I cast out demons and accomplish cures to-day and to-morrow, and on the third day I shall be perfected. . . . You shall not see me until the time when you may say: Blessed is he who comes in the name of the Lord!"

---

[98] Compare the form of this saying in a similar setting, Matt. 16. 27f.

[99] 9. 24. [100] 12. 4. [101] Luke 13. 31ff.

Aside from these words and a few of similar import scattered here and there, Luke does not stress the future aspects of the Reign of God as much as he does the development of a better social order with deeply ethical foundations in the present world.

In the ethical program of the Reign of God Luke sees more and more importance given to personal values, over against the traditional value inherent in conventional usage and ancient institutions. Class consciousness within the Kingdom is subordinate to the instinct of brotherhood. No individualism appeals to this evangelist after his study of the teaching of Jesus, for the law of social amity demands an abiding altruism, subordinating one's property, one's social position, even one's national pride to the ideal of service for others.

The view of the Reign of God in the third Gospel is specific and concrete rather than abstract. Since John Baptist's time the new order has really been in force,[102] hence it is logical to say, "The Reign of God is within you,"[103] although it is not the special privilege of Pharisees nor, indeed, of any one class, to possess it,[104] and all who enjoy its blessings must submit to its conditions.[105]

These conditions involve a degree of inner readiness[106] which will show itself in loving service of others,[107] and in a consistent following of the principles of social amity.[108]

Assignments for Class Reports

1. How do you understand the prophecy of the angel

[102] 16. 16. [103] 17. 21. [104] 13. 28–30.
[105] 13. 1–5. [106] 11. 37–41. [107] 7. 44–48.
[108] 6. 46–49.

of the Annunciation, Luke 1. 32f., in its reference to "the throne of David"?

2. In what way does Jesus' statement about John Baptist in Luke 7. 28 support the view that John's teaching about the new era was a contemporary Jewish view which Jesus repudiated?
3. What probably was the content of the preaching of the Twelve according to Luke 9. 2?
4. Indicate all the parables in the third Gospel which distinctly contribute to our understanding of the Kingdom as Luke understood it.
5. Explain the words ascribed to Jesus in Luke 17. 22–24, paraphrasing them in terms intelligible to the student of to-day.
6. Does Luke mean by his words concerning Joseph of Arimathæa (23. 51), that the latter had been instructed by Jesus? Or does "looking for the Kingdom of God" mean simply that he was a pious Israelite? See Luke 2. 25.

CHAPTER V

THE ETHICS OF THE GOSPEL ACCORDING TO JOHN

The Fourth Gospel Considered as a Source of Ethical Teaching

A single reading of the Gospels informs the student that the last of these books dealing with Jesus and his teaching differs from all the others in many respects. Further study of the Gospel according to John shows conclusively that not only in style, choice of material, and general perspective, but also in aim and purpose, this writer stands apart.

In the synoptic Gospels Jesus talks about the Kingdom of God, uses many parables to illustrate its different aspects, talks very little about himself, but performs many works of mercy upon the needy and takes particular interest in the training of twelve men to carry on his work after his demise.

In the fourth Gospel the phrase "Kingdom of God" scarcely appears, no parables are related by the evangelist, Jesus talks continually about himself, and but few of his many miracles are detailed.

Clearly, the aim and purpose of the evangelist differed from the design that led the other Gospel writers to put their thoughts before their readers. The Fourth Evangelist himself in 20.30f., states that he gathered his material and wrote his book particularly to show that Jesus was Messiah and the Son of God, in the hope that his readers would receive life through their faith in Messiah Jesus.

Such an aim is often characterized as "didactic," in the sense that the treatise defends a certain point clearly stated as its thesis, without being distinctly polemical. Some have seen in the fourth Gospel a polemical writing, taking issue with certain views which seem to its writer contrary to the standard belief of his time, but the evidence for this is not clear. On the other hand, this writer does not seem to be interested in bringing clearly to expression Jesus' thought of a moral program in which his followers should unite. Rather, his dominant interest seems to lie in expounding the personality and the redemptive mission of Jesus. John is interested more in the salvation of the individual than in the reconstruction of society.

The recognition of such a plan in the fourth Gospel might discourage entirely any search for ethical teaching within its twenty-one chapters, but for the fact that certain social contacts between Jesus and the community of his time are detailed and reveal in the mind of the writer some rather important ethical concepts which were without doubt shared by him with other leaders in the church of the fourth Christian generation. So there is some warrant for an inquiry into this later statement of the ethics of Jesus by a writer who lived at Ephesus probably very near the end of the first century, A.D.

About half of the fourth Gospel is taken up with an account of the last week in Jesus' life, thus giving but little space to the ministry in Galilee. The synoptic Gospels offer abundant details of the

Galilæan ministry, but give very little place to Jesus' ministry in Judæa. When it is recalled that in John there is no story of the Temptation, no Transfiguration, no Sermon on the Mount, no agony in the garden of Gethsemane, its different character is felt, for these are cardinal points in the synoptic story.[1]

On the other hand there is much discourse material in the fourth Gospel which has no parallel whatever in the synoptics. The discourse with Nicodemus,[2] the conversation with the Samaritan woman at Jacob's Well,[3] the apologia of Jesus,[4] in which he claims absolute dependence upon the Father, the very mystical statements about the "bread of life," the day after the feeding of the great multitude with a small ration of food,[5] the homily upon the "living water,"[6] which is continued in the discourse upon the "light of the world,"[7] to which should be added the discourse that had as its text the healing of the blind man,[8] constitute characteristic portions of Johannine teaching. Added to these are the still more formal addresses found in chapters ten to seventeen, namely, The Good Shepherd, The Abiding-places with the Father, The Vine and the Branches, The Coming Paraclete or Advocate-helper, The Prayer of Jesus for His Disciples. Other remarkable paragraphs of instruction are found in the story of Lazarus,[9] at the time of the visit of the Greeks,[10] on the occasion of

[1] For a very complete list of omissions from the synoptic account of Jesus' life see D. A. Hayes, *John and His Writings*, pp. 80–88.
[2] John 3. 3–15. [3] 4. 7–26. [4] 5. 19–47.
[5] 6. 22–65. [6] 7. 37ff. [7] 8. 12–20.
[8] 9. 3–5, with the following conversation.
[9] 11. 25ff. [10] 12. 23ff.

the Last Supper,[11] and in the appendix of the Gospel, when after the resurrection Jesus met his disciples in Galilee,[12] and encouraged Peter to continue in his service.

A survey of this teaching of Jesus supports the statement that John did not use to any great extent the discourses of Mark, Luke, and Matthew when he wrote his Gospel. His is not only new material, but it has a different quality.

Assignments for Class Reports

1. After reading all the discourses in the fourth Gospel, indicate four which describe Jesus in some striking way. Offer your own titles for these discourses.
2. Compare the conversations of Jesus in the fourth Gospel with those in Mark, with especial reference to the use of questions.
3. Gather together as many significant words as possible which are used by John and not by the synoptic writers.
4. Investigate the frequency of the words "truth," "love," "life," "believe" in the fourth Gospel.
5. What is the probable date of the Gospel according to John?
6. What persons appear in the fourth Gospel who are not found in the other Gospels?
7. Why is the "pericope adulteræ," 7. 53—8. 11, considered alien to John?

Social Contacts of Jesus in the Fourth Gospel

The first three Gospels present a portrait of Jesus which in no way removes him from intimate and sympathetic contact with all phases of the

[11] 13. 12ff., 31ff. [12] 21. 15–22.

life of his time. Likewise the fourth Gospel, notwithstanding its somewhat different aim, makes very much of the real and constant fellowship which Jesus enjoyed with men and women of many types. If in the synoptics Jesus repeats the insulting words hurled at him, "a gluttonous man and winebibber,"[13] in the fourth Gospel he is found replenishing the supply of wine at a wedding-feast,[14] or holding conversation with a woman whom most Jews would hold in contempt,[15] or walking among a nondescript company of sick and crippled folk, whom many held to be a source of contamination,[16] or again, in serious discussion with a learned man who had come by night to ask the Teacher about his views.[17] In the view of this evangelist, not all the Twelve were of the highest and noblest mind, for Jesus is heard characterizing Judas as "a devil,"[18] as unclean,[19] and as lifting up his heel against his host, in Old Testament phrase,[20] yet how tender is the Master even with this treacherous disciple when they eat for the last time together![21] Jesus had a virile word for each whom he touched. If he came to the house of mourning, both sisters of his own beloved friend could say with greatest confidence, that if their Master had been with them in the illness of Lazarus, his death would not have occurred,[22] and the neighbors, upon seeing the grief of Jesus at the grave, remarked upon his love for his friend.[23] When the Teacher sees a vast concourse of pilgrims approaching him, on one occasion, he begins to counsel with his disciples as to the possibility of

[13] Luke 7. 34. [14] John 2. 1–11. [15] 4. 7–26.
[16] 5. 2–9. [17] 3. 1–15. [18] 6. 70. [19] 13. 11.
[20] 13. 18. [21] 13. 26ff. [22] 11. 21, 32. [23] 11. 36.

finding food for so many.[24] Even when one whom he had befriended was excommunicated from the congregation[25] Jesus still sought him out for further inquiry. And the most remarkable though stray story of his disposal of the case of a woman charged with a breach of moral law[26] makes it clear that both in the synoptics and in John the Master of men and the Teacher of teachers came into vital contact with the life that men live, and that at times he found the unconventional approach most convenient.

It can scarcely be made out that the Fourth Evangelist wrote in order to emphasize these and other social phases of Jesus' life, for his emphasis is primarily upon the exalted character of Jesus as the Messiah and as divine. The very sympathetic outlook of Jesus which does find exposition in this Gospel, however, illustrates how persistently this real side of Jesus continued to characterize the memory and tradition as to his teaching while among his fellows.

The insight which Jesus had into the inner nature of men is vividly portrayed, perhaps in the mind of the Fourth Evangelist, as a supernatural trait of Jesus, yet discernible to the reader as a genuine characteristic of one who "himself knew what was in man."[27] The story of the first disciples of Jesus illustrates finely this keen vision of his. A chance hearing draws two disciples of John Baptist, one of whom was named Andrew, to spend a day with Jesus, with such a consequent interest in him that

[24] John 6. 5. In the synoptics the feeding of the five thousand takes place after they have been for a day with Jesus, but in the fourth Gospel the situation is otherwise described.

[25] 9. 35. [26] 7. 53—8. 11. [27] 2. 25.

they fetch a third, Simon, to whom Jesus gives the surname "Peter" (Rock) as soon as he looks upon him.[28] Another disciple, Philip, Jesus invites to follow him, and Philip in turn brings Nathanael, who comes with a reluctance which disappears when the Master shows that he already knows something about him.[29]

The woman of Samaria tells with astonishment that this prophet opened up her life to her as she supposed only she herself knew it,[30] and urges her fellow townsmen to hear and know him. That this invitation was eagerly accepted is witnessed by the fact that Jesus remained in Samaria two days and convinced these people of his unusual powers. When the statement of the evangelist is recalled that the Jews regularly avoided intercourse with the people of Samaria, this incident speaks eloquently of the remarkable ease with which Jesus approached even the prejudiced and of the equally remarkable insight with which he dealt with the indifferent.

That the evangelist took particular interest in exhibiting this keenness of vision on the part of Jesus appears in his parenthetical statement in the story of the feeding of five thousand,[31] "for he knew what he would do," in his account of the withdrawal of Jesus from the people when their royalistic tendencies become apparent,[32] and in his characterization of the motives of those who sought him out, because they were satisfied with mere bread.[33]

Jesus in the fourth Gospel is fully human in his interests and in his sympathies. He himself knows hunger and fatigue,[34] he experiences indignation at

[28] 1. 42. [29] 1. 48f. [30] 4. 29. [31] 6. 6.
[32] 6. 15. [33] 6. 26. [34] 4. 6ff.

any show of hypocrisy or formality or irreverence,[35] he is appreciative of every act of devotion or service.[36] John portrays Jesus as a teacher who possessed that fine sensibility to human need and human nature which is a prime necessity in a teacher of ethics.

Assignments for Class Reports

1. Paraphrase the story of the first disciples of Jesus in John 1. 35–51.
2. How many times in this Gospel does Jesus refer to "the Twelve"? Are these to be identified with the "disciples" of John 7. 3, or are the latter "the many" spoken of in 2. 23? Find, if possible, the names of twelve disciples in this Gospel.
3. Write a five-hundred word essay upon the social life of Palestine in Jesus' day, using material found only in the fourth Gospel.
4. To what extent is John interested in the economic conditions of the people of Jesus' day? Compare Mark 10. 21; 12. 38ff.; Matt. 9. 36 and similar passages.
5. What element of social service can be found in the Johannine accounts of Jesus' miracles?

The Johannine Way of Expressing the Moral Thought and Program of Jesus

It has appeared in the foregoing pages that the aim of the Fourth Evangelist is other than the detailing of Jesus' moral teaching to his disciples. In fact, the attention of his readers is centered upon the person of Jesus as Messiah and Son of God, not particularly as a sponsor of a new order which should be characterized by a vigorous propaganda

[35] 2. 15ff.; 11. 33 margin. [36] 12. 8; 18. 9–11.

in accordance with a program set forth by the Master himself.

One searches in vain for a Johannine counterpart to the Sermon on the Mount, for such specific directions to Jesus' followers as are found in Matthew 10 and Luke 9 and 10, for exhortations as to brothers who need forgiveness such as are set forth in Matthew 18, or for such condemnation of the materially minded as Luke offers in many of his parables.

John Baptist, it is true, appears as a teacher of righteousness in the fourth Gospeal, but here he does not reprove a Herod nor does he give moral instruction to the several classes of penitents before him. Jesus does not warn his hearers of the scribes who "devour widows' houses," he does not charge any man to give up his wealth, he raises no such large moral issue as that of divorce, he gives no advice as to tribute to Cæsar.

In the Gospel according to John one finds the moral thought of Jesus recast into such sublime concepts as "truth," "love," "life," "light," with their opposites. This is not to say that John is altogether abstract rather than concrete and objective, for the performance of one's duty is plainly made the basis of certainty in the ethical life of men. "If anyone is willing to do his will, he shall know concerning the teaching, whether it is from God or whether I speak in my own right."[37] At the Last Supper Jesus put his friends to a practical test involving unselfish service, when he himself took the attitude of a servant and washed their feet,

---

[37] 7. 17; compare 13. 35; 14. 15; 15. 12.

assuring them that they had no real part with him if they did not share this spirit of willingness to serve.

This evangelist takes some account of actual breach of the moral law on the part of the enemies of Jesus, whom he usually characterizes as "the Jews." Their intention of killing Jesus is several times pointed out with condemnation.[38] and the highly immoral act of Judas Iscariot[39] is scathingly rebuked.

The Sabbath question appears in this Gospel, but not with the same emphasis as in the synoptics. The breaking of the Sabbath is noted,[40] but the evangelist thinks that it is the alleged blasphemy of Jesus rather than the desecration of the day itself that aroused the anger of the Jews. The man who was restored to health is chided for carrying his bed on the Sabbath,[41] but the complaint is directed back toward Jesus, who told him to take up his bed and walk. The Pharisees, it is true, argued that Jesus was an impostor because of his disregard of the Sabbath,[42] but some of the more fair-minded among them felt that the remarkable deeds which Jesus performed were favorable to his character.

The moral code in its objective demands receives further notice in John at the time of the Temple cleansing, when Jesus demanded of the traders that they cease to make his Father's house a place of business. Here, however, the accusation which figures in each of the synoptic stories of the cleansing, "You have made it a den of robbers," is absent.

---

[38] For example, 7. 19; 8. 37, 40; 10. 31ff.
[39] 13. 21; 18. 3; 6. 70.
[40] 5. 9b–18. [41] 5. 10. [42] 9. 16.

The tremendous religious zeal of Jesus is emphasized in the Johannine version of this Messianic act:

"His disciples recalled that it is written,
Zeal for thy house shall consume me."[43]

Aside from the comparatively few instances above noted, and these with the modifications that appear by comparison with the synoptic method, the Johannine way of expressing Jesus' moral thought is through the use of high ethical concepts which, at the close of the first Christian century, at least for the church in Asia Minor, have taken the place of the more practical and concrete precepts of the synoptics.

In the prolog of the Gospel, Jesus is described as "the true light, which illuminates every man coming into the world."[44]

After the Johannine method of antithesis, the light is contrasted with darkness, and Jesus declares that he himself is "the light of the world,"[45] the context in each case leaving no doubt in the reader's mind that the evangelist has in mind the pursuit of a highly moral program in life.[46]

The concept "light" thus suggests that of "life," which is found frequently in this Gospel,[47] and which forms an important vehicle of expression for the developing concept of the Reign of God. The fullest exposition of this term will find place more appropriately in the next section, devoted to the Johannine teaching as to the Kingdom of God.

[43] John 2. 17. [44] 1. 9. [45] 8. 12; 12. 46.

[46] Note 12. 47, "If any man hear my sayings and does not keep them," and in 8. 12 compare the use of "life" with the use of this term in 1. 4, "In him was life, and the life was the light of men."

[47] The word for "life" occurs more than thirty times in this Gospel. The word for "light" occurs at least twenty-two times, nearly twice as frequently as in the synoptics.

Here the student's interest lies particularly in the use of such a term as "life" to express to the evangelist's readers the thought of Jesus in respect to the life that men live together, insofar as their individual and community life reflects to the evangelist's times the ethical ideals of the man of Galilee.

In 17.3 there is a statement which sounds more like a definition of the term: "And this is eternal life, that they may know thee, the only true God, and him whom thou didst send, Jesus Christ."

It is life indeed to know the only true God. With Mark[48] the Kingdom ideal involved the development of fine ethical relations between men and men and between men and God. With Matthew,[49] the thought of a likeness to the Father ("sons of your Father") was more clearly developed than with Mark. With John, the thought of personal fellowship with the Father is daringly set forth in such words as, "I am the way, and the truth, and the life; no one comes to the Father except through me,"[50] and "He who has my commandments and keeps them, this man is one who loves me. . . . And he shall be beloved of my Father,"[51] There is also emphasis upon the relation between Jesus and the disciple, which the synoptists taught. "By this shall all men know that you are my disciples," said Jesus, "if you love one another."[52] As a condition of continuance in the life of a disciple the Master said: "If you love me keep my commandments."[53] In these sayings, the life that is lived is closely associated with the brotherly attitude,

[48] Pages 70–75 above, "Ethical Relations between Persons in the Kingdom."
[49] Page 100 above.
[50] 14. 6. [51] 14. 21. [52] 13. 35. [53] 14. 15.

sympathetic and affectionate, denoted by the Johannine word "love."

The statement of 17.3 above quoted is found in the prayer which Jesus prayed shortly before his death. In the context it appears that the great Teacher realized that his work on earth was finished, yet his friends must continue to live and work and achieve under those very human conditions in which they found themselves. The Father is not to take them out of the world,[54] yet their life that they live is to be in a certain degree of contrast to the life of the world. The unity which the company of disciples must possess[55] is to be a personal unity comprising the Father and Jesus himself and the disciples. And this unity is to involve yet others, not of the original band. This presupposes a program of activity on their part[56] which is very clearly implicit throughout the Gospel.[57]

The concept "light," which merges into that of "life" in so many places in the fourth Gospel, is seen in some of the passages above quoted to dissolve again into the concept "love," a favorite word with this evangelist.[58] In the discourse upon the Vine and its Branches[59] Jesus said: "This is my commandment, that you love one another just as I loved you." As if in further exposition of love as a moral principle, these words follow: "Greater love than this no man possesses, that one should lay down his life for his friends." Jesus'

[54] 17. 15. [55] 17. 21. [56] 17. 20.
[57] 1. 8; 3. 14–16; 4. 39–42; 6. 45; 10. 16; 12. 19, 46; and similar passages.
[58] The verb "to love" is used at least forty-four times in John's Gospel; the noun "love" is used seven times. There are two different verbs used, one being used thirty-four times, the other ten.
[59] 15. 12.

own example is supreme, as the evangelist has already expressed it in the words,[60] "Having loved his own in the world, he loved them to the end."

In another place[61] Jesus referred to the commandment to love one another as "a new commandment," and here also made the measure of his own love for the disciples the standard for love of one another in the moral community.

The fourth Gospel is the latest of all, and behind it lies a longer stretch of moral experience for the followers of Jesus. That very experience had brought to these valiant souls many shafts of light to illuminate their way, perhaps at unexpected turns, in fulfillment of the words which this evangelist writes of the Spirit of Truth: "And when he comes, the spirit of truth, he will lead you in all truth."[62]

The actual words of Jesus could not offer, even if they were all written down,[63] complete provision for all the future needs of the disciples. But experience taught all the evangelists that a personal fellowship would be established between the still living Teacher and his followers, which should indeed provide for all exigencies. This personal experience of the living Jesus John designates in various ways, the clearest of all perhaps being his manner of using the words, "light," "life," "love," "truth."

Assignments for Class Reports

1. Follow the word "life" in the fourth Gospel, using a Concordance, and report all instances of its use which clearly refer to the moral program in which the followers of Jesus unite.

---

[60] 13. 1. [61] 13. 34. [62] 16. 13. [63] John 20. 30; 21. 25.

2. Paraphrase John 16. 1–13, bringing to expression the various moral attitudes implicit in the passage.
3. Compare the use of the words "life," "light," "love," "truth" in the fourth Gospel with their use in the synoptics. Note relative frequency as well as different words for similar English translations.

The Kingdom of God in the Fourth Gospel

The phrase "Kingdom of God" appears but twice in the fourth Gospel, namely, in 3. 3, 5, both times on the lips of Jesus. Again, thrice in 18. 36, Jesus uses the expression "my kingdom" in addressing Pontius Pilate. Aside from these instances, the expression, so frequently met in the synoptic Gospels, does not occur in John.

In Jesus' use of the term "kingdom" before Pilate's judgment bar one finds practically a denial that the Kingdom of God is at home upon earth. "My kingdom is not of this world. If my kingdom were of this world, then would my followers strive against my betrayal to the Jews. But now my kingdom is not from hence."

To Nicodemus Jesus said: "Unless one be born from above one cannot see the Kingdom of God." Then more explicitly, "Unless one be born of water and of the spirit, one cannot enter the Kingdom of God."

When the term "Kingdom of God" is used so sparingly it may be questioned whether the writer of this Gospel held the idea which underlies the term in the synoptic Gospels. At least his Gospel must be investigated carefully with a view to learning whether John had dismissed the idea of the present or the coming Kingdom or whether he had modified it, or whether possibly he holds the same view on the whole, although he does not prize the synoptists' term for the new order taught by them.

One of the first things to meet the student engaged in such an investigation will be the prominence given by John to belief in Jesus himself as a condition of discipleship, if not even as a condition of personal salvation. With the Fourth Evangelist this faith is directed more toward the person of Jesus than toward his message. John Baptist witnessed to Jesus that all men "through him might believe,"[64] the evangelist declares that God sent Jesus into the world for the purpose of bringing all to believe on him,[65] and Jesus repeatedly associates belief in himself with faith in the Father, "who sent him."[66] The individual believer seems to be pointed out particularly by the Fourth Evangelist, and this interest in the individual probably accounts for the absence of specific teaching as to a moral community, its mutual obligations and laws.

Even the group known as "the Twelve" is not as prominent in this Gospel as in the synoptics. Once the number is mentioned, namely 6. 70,

"Did I not choose you, the twelve? And of you one is a devil."

At the Last Supper the number is not named, the general term "the disciples"[67] being used. Where the synoptists emphasize the number of the twelve, (the number is twice mentioned by each in the account of the Supper), one finds the statement of Jesus in John 13. 21, "One of you shall betray me." John indicates that those who followed Jesus were

---

[64] 1. 7. [65] 3. 16; 20. 31.
[66] 6. 29; 12. 44; 14. 7, 9; 17. 11. [67] 13. 5.

numerous. He had "more disciples than John Baptist,"[68] "many believed" when he was at Jerusalem,[69] "many more believed" than the Samaritan woman,[70] when Jesus spent two days at Sychar, in fact, many even of the religious leaders believed on Jesus, although they dared not become openly his followers.[71]

The readers of John's Gospel would not hesitate to associate this group of believers, not all of whom were in one "fold,"[72] with the larger group of believers who constituted the very churches in which this Gospel had its first circulation. Thus the Christian of the fourth generation after Jesus would accept as a correct designation for himself the terms "born of God" and "son of God,"[73] as well as the term "disciple" or "believer." Whatever was affirmed of the first disciples would apply to those who were numbered among Jesus' followers at the end of the first century.

In the terms that he chooses the Fourth Evangelist does not make clear to his reader that the Kingdom of God is a moral program which is being carried on by the believers in Jesus, for in the few places where the name is explicitly used an earthly environment is not demanded. One must be "born from above," or "born of water and of Spirit," even to enter the Kingdom of God. Yet in his conversation with Nicodemus, Jesus refers to these very statements, with others, as having to do with "earthly things,"[74] in contrast with the "heavenly things" which Nicodemus was not prepared to understand. Thus,[75] "unless one is born of water

[68] 4. 1. [69] 2. 23. [70] 4. 41. [71] 12. 42f.
[72] 10. 16. [73] 1. 12, 13. [74] 3. 12. [75] 3. 5.

and of Spirit," one cannot enter the Kingdom. Again,[76] one who is "born of spirit" is likened to the wind, particularly stressing its invisibility and its mystery. These terms, however, do not as fully identify the ethical program of the Kingdom with earthly affairs as Matthew does in the Sermon on the Mount. The Fourth Evangelist seems partial to expressions which turn the attention of his reader away from the workaday world. These words he puts on the lips of Jesus,[77] in one of his most important conversations with his disciples:

> "The spirit is the life-giver; the flesh does no good. The words which I have spoken to you are spirit and they are life."

Despite this emphasis upon the spiritual as over against the temporal, this last Gospel teaches that the disciple of Jesus is one of a cherished group whose members live in the midst of an unfriendly world,[78] yet who enjoy the advantage of the unseen support of an influential personal Advocate,[79] who will reveal to them coming values and who will remain a constant personal Counselor in the stead of their departed Master.

The message of the sixteenth chapter of John together with that of the fourteenth must have been understood by the first readers of the Gospel as direct encouragement in their efforts to carry forward the program of Jesus, including an aggressive propaganda in Asia Minor. One can scarcely affirm, then, in view of this portion of the fourth Gospel, that the moral community made up of Jesus' followers, is not included in the Kingdom of God. But all the evidence to be marshaled on both

[76] 3. 8. [77] 6. 63. [78] 16. 1–4. [79] 16. 7, 13.

It is true that in a few cases the "life" of which John speaks is a living beyond the sphere of this world's activities,[92] and one has a right to expect that a type of experience which merits the term "eternal life" must survive the temporal values of this existence. The largest number of instances, however, in which the term is used must refer to the life of the followers of Jesus in the world that now is.

The Kingdom of God is thus still a vital concept in the mind of this latest evangelist, although he does not see fit to repeat the term frequently. He understands that the life within the community whose nucleus consisted of the first intimate friends and students of Jesus and whose extent was, in his own time, well-nigh empire wide, is in reality the personal life of Jesus, still present within the Christian community, even though no longer in the flesh. "It is the spirit that gives life."

Assignments for Class Reports

1. Investigate the frequency with which the term "Kingdom of God" occurs in Paul's writings, in Mark, in John's Apocalypse. Note the dates of these writings and compare this usage with that in the synoptics and in the fourth Gospel. What conclusions can you draw from the data obtained?
2. Write an exposition of the fifteenth chapter of John's Gospel, pointing out particularly its ethical teaching.
3. Paraphrase John 6. 26–40.
4. Investigate the use of the word "salvation" in each of the four Gospels. To what extent is the Johannine view of salvation strictly ethical?

[92] For example, 5. 29; 10. 28; 12. 25.

CHAPTER VI

THE ETHICS OF THE GOSPELS AND THE ETHICS OF JESUS

The Problem of Identifying the Ethical Teaching of Jesus When Only Secondary Sources Are At Hand

At least four men in the early church who were sympathetic with that movement known first as The Way and later as Christianity left to posterity their views of Jesus' teaching as that teaching was held in their time and place. In the foregoing pages the work of these men has been studied inductively, with a view to finding in each case the important elements of early Christian ethics.

No writing from the pen of Jesus exists. A few Aramaic words are found imbedded in the Gospels, transliterated and in some cases explained by a corresponding Greek word.[1] But no modern student may expect to look upon any primary source of the Master's teaching. The Gospels stand as the only reliable sources of that original teaching.

If it were true that Jesus' teaching was entirely new and wholly original in content as well as in form, then the student might well doubt whether a successful attempt could ever be made to restore the oral teaching of the Galilæan prophet from the

[1] Among these are Raca, Matt. 5. 22; Beelzebub (Beelzebul), Matt. 10. 25; 12. 24, 27; Luke 11. 15 et al.; Talitha cumi, Mark 5. 41; Ephphatha, Mark 7. 34; Abba, Mark 14. 36 and Eli, Eli, lama sabachthani? Mark 15. 34; Matt. 27. 46.

written records of a generation or two after his death. The evangelists themselves, however, do not assure their readers that the teaching of Jesus was something overwhelmingly new and unrelated to the contemporary ethical teaching of Judaism. Matthew adds to his form of the Golden Rule,[2] "for this is the law and the prophets." Mark points out that Jesus directed the attention of the wealthy inquirer[3] to the Decalog when asked, "What shall I do to inherit eternal life?" Luke indicates approval by the Master of the Jewish scribe who cited the words of Deut. 6. 4 and Lev. 19. 18 as the substance of high moral endeavor. Jesus said to the scribe: "Do this and you shall live."[4]

The evangelists assure their readers that Jesus repeatedly appealed to the prophets of the eighth and seventh centuries before his time with high approval.[5] There is good reason to suppose that Jesus read other Jewish books than those found in the law and the prophets, books which reflected the moral thinking of enlightened men of the few generations immediately preceding him. Among these books were probably the wisdom book of the son of Sirach (Ecclesiasticus), The Testaments of the Twelve Patriarchs and others, including many contemporary Pharisaic writings and a number of apocalypses.

While the evangelists appear to vary between themselves in their interest in the universal spread of the Kingdom, they are all agreed that the moral community taught by the Master took its rise within

---

[2] Matt. 7. 12. [3] Mark 10. 17ff. [4] Luke 10. 25-27.
[5] See Matt. 5. 17; 9. 13; 12. 18ff.; 13. 14ff.; 15. 8f.; Luke 4. 18-21 and similar places. Review pages 58-60 above.

Judaism and that its cardinal principles were not other than those which experience had taught to be morally sound.

The historical approach to the problem as to Jesus' original teaching thus finds a substantial element of that teaching in the tried and true moral principles of the great teachers of Judaism. For by analogy with later development in moral thinking and ethical codes it must be that no abrupt break with prevalent moral thought could be tolerated by one who looked upon Judaism as his ancestral religion and who sought, prophetlike, to rid that religion of immoral theory and practice.

Fortunately, much research has been made within the realm of Jewish moral teaching, thus offering the student a very abundant and well-certified mass of material with which to reconstruct the moral environment into which Jesus came.[6] This relatively recent interest in the Jewish background of the Lord's teaching has done much to stimulate the historical study of the teaching of Jesus as found in the Gospels, with the result that the essentials of Jesus' own teaching are better certified than ever before.[7]

An assured result of such investigation is the conviction that in the case of Christian ethics there was noticeable development within the first few generations. It may be shown, in fact, that during

---

[6] Notable among these works are Thomas Walker, *The Teaching of Jesus and the Jewish Teaching of His Age;* J. M. P. Smith, *The Moral Life of the Hebrews;* H. G. Mitchell, *Ethics of the Old Testament;* G. Friedlaender, *Jewish Sources of the Sermon on the Mount.*

[7] The student is referred to such recent works as those of E. F. Scott, *The Ethical Teaching of Jesus;* A. C. Headlam, *The Life and Teaching of Jesus the Christ;* E. I. Bosworth, *The Life and Teaching of Jesus.*

the first three generations of Christian believers there was a more rapid and vital development in moral thinking than in many similar periods before or after. The words of the Fourth Evangelist; "Remember the word that I said to you, a servant is not greater than his master,"[8] are charged with the meaning that new light often came to the disciple as he "remembered" such words. The statement as to the Paraclete, "He shall guide you in all truth"[9] implies strongly that during the intervening years the followers of Jesus had learned new things concerning right living which the Master had not explicitly taught.

These conclusions carry with them certain implications. Since no evangelist was aware that he was writing a Bible portion, but, rather, was persuaded that his message was designed for a particular person or group of his acquaintance, each writer of Jesus' life or words felt free to edit even the written accounts that came to his hand. Luke admits that many others had attempted such written accounts,[10] and he himself noticeably depends upon the earlier account of Mark, yet he feels free to omit the narrative of Jesus' visit to the regions of Tyre and Sidon, the feeding of the four thousand, and other very interesting episodes from his own narrative. Matthew likewise feels free to omit many questions from Jesus' lips as found in Mark, although there is excellent evidence to show that Mark's account formed the basis of the first Gospel.[11]

---

[8] John 15. 20. [9] John 16. 13. [10] Luke 1. 1.
[11] Allen, "Saint Matthew," *International Critical Commentary*, p. xxxii, offers eleven instances of such omission, apparently on principle.

Sometimes these changes appear to be the result of some principle, perhaps the rise of a higher degree of reverence for the Twelve, which in the day of the First Evangelist led him to leave out some words which seemed to him below the dignity of these apostles. In other instances an adaptation of the message to his circle of readers is clear. In illustration of the latter Mark 10. 12 may be cited. Here the Second Evangelist includes a case that is allowed by Roman law, the divorcing of a husband by a wife. Mark is writing for Roman readers. But in Palestine, where no woman had the right to divorce her husband, the original words probably did not embrace such a supposed case.

The problem of reaching the original teaching of Jesus is thus by no means hopeless, although too great a degree of optimism and assurance should not sway the student. He has at hand the well-tested literary and historical principles which have wrought well in this field and in others. He has also at hand fairly well certified copies of the Greek Gospels, with many competing readings, yet with no very essential variation. The student finds encouragement in the present high degree of assurance that the evangelists were sympathetic with the movement whose rise they chronicle, and in at least one case, that of Luke, there is excellent assurance of his character as a careful and accurate recorder of details as his sources bring them to him.

The inductive study of all four Gospels brings still further confidence that there is no vital contradiction between any two writers as to the nature of Jesus' teaching, although each writer uses his own style, shapes his message for his own constituency, edits his material as he finds desirable, and often expresses his own views, which may in no real sense be a part of the express teaching of Jesus.

To one who is able successfully to adopt the point of view of the writers and first readers of these Gospels there is a high degree of expectation possible in apprehending the original message of Jesus. Such an achievement results from a consistent use of a knowledge of the times and their needs, from an application of the law of probability as based on a knowledge of the psychology of the Oriental and from that wider knowledge of the total development of moral thought within the Jewish Church and the Christian Church of the first three or four generations.

The Sayings of Jesus

Early writers in the Christian Church felt a degree of certainty in regard to the genuine sources of the four Gospels, and statements from some of these writers embody a tradition that Peter and other eyewitnesses of the Lord's ministry were responsible for the sayings of Jesus found in such number in the works of the evangelists. Luke makes special mention of written sources to which he had access[12] and in all the Gospels there is implicit testimony to the existence of a somewhat wealthy store of sayings which had been passed on from mouth to mouth for a greater or shorter time before the teaching thus transmitted orally was incorporated in one or another of the written accounts of Jesus' life.

---

[12] Luke I. 1–4.

If in preceding chapters the student has become impressed with the fact that he has at hand only secondary sources, namely, the writings of men of a generation or two after Jesus, he may still be reassured that such an impression is doubtless true to the literary situation. At this point, however, it will be well to call attention to some of the original elements in the Gospels, which appear to bring one very close indeed to the spoken word of Jesus himself.

Certain principles of literary criticism aid one who seeks to identify those sayings that have been least affected by the process of their transmission. These principles are to be invoked also in the following section in exhibiting the manner in which some of the teaching of Jesus has been modified or expanded by this same process of transmission. Not all the original sayings can be identified, by any means, nor can all the modifications or expansions of the teaching be traced. Still there is sufficient evidence to establish both types of teaching, namely, the relatively unchanged oral teaching of Jesus and the literary work done by the evangelists upon much of the teaching.[13]

Each evangelist has a style of his own. This can be readily identified and has been pointed out in each case by life-long students of the Gospels. In many places where the three synoptic writers have made use of the same material each evangelist has

---

[13] The limitations of this work render it impossible to go at length into the question of sources of the Gospels and equally impossible to make an exhaustive catalog of the sayings that can be identified. The method here pointed out should be useful in completing such a study, however.

modified or edited that material after his own way.[14] But in other places where three, or two or one of the synoptic writers have used material from their sources they have left it apparently in the form in which they found it. This form may then be ascribed to the compiler or editor of some literary source now lost, or to the speaker of the words himself. In the case of sayings orally transmitted one must make allowance for the accidents of translation from one language to another, for example, from Aramaic to Greek, thence to English, yet in substance the style of the transmitted saying may not be essentially changed. It is in this relatively unaltered mass of sayings that one is certain to find the most nearly primitive or original material.

In his teaching Jesus appears to use the method of Socrates very frequently. In the second Gospel many instances of the question are on Jesus' lips. If some of these questions are suppressed by another evangelist who used the second Gospel, it can be shown that this is to be accounted for by an editorial process, the evangelist being influenced by his own view that to ask many questions, some of them apparently for the acquisition of information, did not befit the Messiah.

One of the oldest sources of the Gospels may be found in the document used by Luke, especially in chapters 9 to 18. Here is a large block of discourse material, in the form of parables, table-talk, and occasional conversations. No doubt may reasonably be held that in this primitive source is found the form of Jesus' sayings as well as much of their sub-

[14] The following section will offer detailed illustrations of such practice.

stance. It is not likely that the Master indulged in extensive lectures or sermons. Rather, he used each opportunity that offered itself for illustration of the principles of right living and character development which filled his thought.

In the light of the foregoing, those words of Jesus found in the Gospels which have a pithy, quotable form are likely to be a part of that tradition which has preserved the essence of the unforgettable sentences uttered in conversation, in repartee, in challenge to hesitating or doubting disciples or in withering criticism of adversaries.

For illustration note such sayings as "You are the salt of the earth. . . . You are the light of the world."[15] The former has an echo in Mark 5. 34, "Salt is good," not, of course, a parallel but another saying altogether. Again, "Come to me, all who are laboring and are heavy laden and I will give you ease; take my yoke upon you and learn of me, for I am of a meek and lowly spirit, and you shall find rest for your souls,"[16] appearing in no parallel place, bears in its form good evidence of originality. In the synoptics generally Jesus is not represented as talking much about himself, but much about God and about right living. This exceptional passage does not take its form from any recognized Matthæan literary trait, nor from the thesis of the Gospel itself. It breathes rather directly the spirit of the Prophet of Nazareth himself, as that spirit is revealed under the literary forms of the several evangelists and through their own chosen aims in writing.

An illustration from the so-called "triple tra-

[15] Matt. 5. 13f. [16] Matt. 11. 28–30.

dition" occurs in the parallels to Mark 10. 31, exactly reproduced in Matt. 19. 30, with the exception of "the" before the second "last," also reversed in order in Matt. 20. 16, which order corresponds to the saying in Luke 13. 30, as shown in the following:

Matthew	*Mark*	*Luke*
"And many first shall be last and last first." (19. 30.) "Thus the last shall be first and the first last." (20. 16.)	"And many first shall be last and the last first." (10. 31.)	"And lo, there are last who shall be first, and there are first who shall be last." (13. 30.)

Aside from the nature of the sayings just illustrated, there is a significance in the discovery that Matthew especially uses the same saying frequently in at least two different contexts. These "doublets" may well be original sayings of Jesus now found in other than the original setting. Such a familiar passage, for example, as the Lord's Prayer occurs in two Gospels in quite different contexts, namely, in Matt. 6. 9ff. and in Luke 11. 1ff. A comparative study of the Beatitudes in Matthew 5 and in Luke 6 will reveal some doublets but more differences than similarities. It is probably impossible now to determine whether the original saying with Jesus was "Happy are you poor," "Happy are the poor," or "Happy are the poor in spirit." But in Matthew occur some remarkable doublets which seem to point to an original form of the words, while the context or occasion of the saying remains in doubt. Take, for example, the saying: "He that endures to the end, the same shall be saved,"[17] once used in the address to the Twelve in Galilee, again in the apocalyptic words spoken on the Mount of

[17] Matt. 10. 22b.; 24. 13.

Olives. Again, the words, "There shall be the weeping and the gnashing of teeth," occur in the application of the story of the talents and in connection with Jesus' commendation of the faith of the centurion of Capernaum.[18] Other interesting doublets of a similar character occur.[19]

The style of Jesus as a speaker was no doubt influenced by the style of the Scriptures in which he was instructed. There are certainly many quotations from the Old Testament which are his own citations from Holy Writ as he addressed the multitudes. But also there are to be found words placed by the evangelists upon Jesus' lips which bear the Old Testament form of parallelism, just as other words bear the form of the Beatitude, so frequently found in the Jewish Scriptures. The following "words of Jesus" are couched in the parallel or balanced measure so often encountered in Proverbs, Psalms and other Old Testament or intertestamental books.

"The healthy have no need of a physician, but those who are ill."[20] "The disciple is not above his teacher, nor the slave above his lord."[21] "And whosoever shall exalt himself shall be humbled and whosoever shall humble himself shall be exalted."[22]

[18] 8. 12b; 25. 30.

[19] The following are suggested for study: Matt. 18. 8–9 compare 5. 30, 29; 12. 39 compare 16. 4; 10. 15 compare 11. 24; 10. 39 compare 16. 25; 16. 19b compare 18. 18; 17. 20 compare 21. 21; 25. 29 compare 13. 12; 24. 42 compare 25. 13.

[20] Matt. 9. 12, compare also Mark 2. 17 and Luke 5. 31.

[21] Matt. 10. 24.

[22] Matt. 23. 12, and note the persistence of this saying in Matt. 18. 4; Luke 14. 11 and 18. 14. The Beatitudes possess this rhythmic form to a remarkable degree. See also such sayings as Matt. 5. 22, 38–42, 43–46; 16. 24–25; Mark 6. 4; 10. 29–30; 12. 38–40; Luke 7. 28; 8. 10; 9. 50; 10. 20; 11. 39; 12. 33–34; 13. 32; 14. 11; 18. 29–30; 21. 3–4; 22. 42 and many others.

Some of Jesus' sayings in the Gospel stand quite loosely connected, if connected at all in sense with their context. This phenomenon, from a literary point of view, may be explained possibly by the supposition that some accident happened to the manuscript at an early date. Or it may be supposed that the compiler of the Gospel saw some connection which is not now apparent to an Occidental, twentieth-century reader. A very possible explanation is to be found in the theory that these semi-detached sayings occur in their original form, representing a part of the teaching of Jesus which has been unaltered yet whose context is entirely lost even to the evangelist. It is to him so obviously a part of the actual discourse of Jesus that he insists upon including it in his written work even though its setting is partly unharmonious.

The student has already noted that Matthew incorporates the Lord's Prayer in the Sermon on the Mount at the expense of a disarrangement of the symmetrical arrangement of the discourse, a symmetry in which that evangelist delighted. So Luke introduces into chapter 12 of his Gospel the words, so clearly original with the Master, "Fear not, little flock, for your Father is pleased to give you the Kingdom."[23]

The saying may be suggested by the reference to the Kingdom in verse 31, "seek his kingdom," but the connection of verse 33 with 32 is most difficult to ascertain.

More striking than this example is the saying on divorce, Luke 16. 18. There is no possible logical connection before or after these words, yet the

[23] Luke 12. 32. See Bruce, *The Kingdom of God*, p. 118.

logion itself is unmistakably like other declarations in Mark and Matthew, which, apart from the restrictive clause in Matthew 5. 32 and 19. 9, are subject to no debate as to their originality.

Another passage, also from the third Gospel, which bears strong marks of originality and yet which is very loosely connected with its literary setting, is Luke 9. 49–50:

> "And John answered, saying, Master, we saw a certain man casting out demons in thy name, and we forbade him, because he did not follow with us. And Jesus said to him, Forbid not; for he who is not against us is for us."

The passage occurs also in Mark 9. 38–40, where the preceding context is like that of Luke, although the following context in Mark seems to relate the logion somewhat to the incident of the child.[24] In Luke, however, 9. 51 marks the beginning of the so-called "long insertion,"[25] which has no parallel in the other Gospels.

Not too much weight should be attached to the existence of such sayings loosely connected with their context in an attempt to show that these detached logia are like "pebbles washed up and left on the shore of the stream of tradition," with no possibility of ever finding the place from which they were wrenched, but in connection with all the considerations above offered, this literary item should have some weight.

To sum up what has been said in regard to the nearly original elements of Jesus' teaching, it appears that the Gospel writers, although differing

---

[24] Mark 9. 36f.; Luke 9. 47f. [25] 9. 51—18. 14.

between themselves in style, in word choice, in aims, and in their circle of readers, have incorporated much discourse or conversation material in its original form. This appears not so much from the fact that such material is found in twofold or threefold tradition,—that is, in two or three parallel places in the Gospels—as from the character of the sayings, from their relation to their context or contexts when they appear as "doublets," and from the style of the sayings considered as a body, apart from the style of the several evangelists.

These men were within a generation or two of Jesus' time. Mark at least enjoyed the intimacy of a chief apostle, and Luke acknowledges his indebtedness to sources, most of which were doubtless in writing. Matthew abounds most of all in "doublets" and thus lays himself liable to the assertion that he placed his material in artificial settings, to serve best his purposes in writing. Luke offers much teaching material not found in the other synoptics. Yet a study of the material incorporated in this "synoptic tradition" seems bound to result in the conviction that the "logia of Jesus," as an early tradition terms these sayings of the Lord, are not far from the reader of the Gospel pages.

Freedom of arrangement was the evangelists' privilege. Chronological accuracy was not sought, nor even desired, by the writers, and no one of them set out to write a life of Jesus. But each in his own way set out to tell a particular story out of that most remarkable life and in doing so each man accurately and vividly portrayed to his readers the spirit of the Great Teacher, the character of his supreme self-sacrifice in behalf of men whom he loved, and the essence of his words which became richer in ethical portent with the years. No earnest student of the Gospels need doubt that the Prophet of Nazareth speaks rather directly through his sympathetic interpreter, the evangelist.

The Evangelists and the Words of Jesus

In the foregoing section an attempt was made to identify the words most nearly original with Jesus. There was found reason to suppose that even when the Gospel writer permitted words of the Teacher to lose their original form he still preserved their thought as he understood it. It has further appeared that in many cases Jesus' words came to a writer with no context or with one not original.

At this point it will be fitting to turn some attention to the freedom which the evangelists used in their disposition of Jesus' teaching and to inquire not only as to the extent of that freedom but also as to its warrant in the minds of the Christian writers and possibly of their readers. First of all, the purpose of a writer, the needs of his circle of readers and his own view of Jesus and his teaching greatly influenced his choice and disposition of narrative and discourse material.

The Fourth Evangelist writes to support the thesis that Jesus is Messiah and that he is Son of God. From the beginning to the end of his work this thesis is prominent. In order to present Jesus as Messiah in the most effective manner, John takes an outstanding Messianic act of the Master, namely, his ridding the Temple of its profiteering traders, and places it at the very beginning of his story.

Along with it is the account of a miracle, which is a "sign" of Jesus' Messiahship, the miracle of turning water to wine. The probable historical position of the Temple cleansing is at the close of the ministry and all three synoptics agree in placing it at the beginning of Passion Week. The thesis of neither synoptic writer demands that the episode be taken out of its historical position. No criticism need be brought against John because he exercised this freedom in replacing the Temple cleansing, just as no criticism of his emphasis upon the Judæan ministry of Jesus is in place. Each Gospel writer exercised equal freedom when his aim demanded it.

The Fourth Evangelist seems now and then to offer comments and interpretations upon words of Jesus, often in such a way that it is quite impossible to tell where, even in the writer's intention, the words of Jesus end and the writer's comments begin. John 3. 16 is often quoted as Jesus' words, but these words may form the beginning of an extensive comment of the writer, including 3. 16–21, to which perhaps 3. 31–36 should be added. In a number of places the evangelist indicates that he is offering a comment, as in 6. 64b: "For Jesus knew from the beginning who they were who did not believe." Again, the writer inserts a well-marked affidavit, as 19. 35; "An eyewitness has testified and true is his testimony." Or he offers explanations of Jesus' words, in such places as 2. 22; 7. 39; 11. 51–53; 12. 16; 19. 28a.

The synoptic writers are in general agreed as to the course and the content of Jesus' ministry and teaching. But this unanimity does not extend to details, and in places agreement gives way to variation or even to contradiction.

In general, there is greater agreement between Mark and Matthew than between any other two writers. Almost all of Mark can be found within the First Gospel. Yet here and there it is possible to find places in which the differing view of Jesus' person or of his work leads to a revision of the saying, to a suppression of detail or again to expansion of a thought. Matthew does not find the narrative of Peter's sorry attempt to walk upon the water of the lake in Mark, his narrative source, notwithstanding Peter is believed to be Mark's chief source of information.[26] On the other hand, Matthew omits Mark's narrative of the healing of a deaf and dumb man,[27] perhaps because the First Evangelist would hesitate to include a story in which Jesus made a second attempt before his cure was complete. This involves a way of thinking about Jesus which in Matthew's time and place was somewhat different from that which prevailed in the Roman church in Mark's time.[28]

Illustrative of individual coloring of the same episode are two found in the Marcan and Matthæan versions of the healing of the demoniac who lived in the tombs and in the cursing of the fig tree.

In the first of these two narratives Matthew tells of two men possessed with demons[29] while

[26] The parallel accounts are found in Matt. 14. 22–33 and Mark 6. 45–52.

[27] Mark 7. 32–37, and note 8. 22–25.

[28] Allen, "St. Matthew," *International Critical Commentary*, p. xxxi, offers many striking changes due to "an increased feeling of reverence for the person of Christ."

[29] Matt. 8. 28–34.

Mark[30] tells of only one. In the second illustration[31] the First Evangelist greatly condenses the story and intensifies it by the statement, "The fig-tree withered immediately," while, according to Mark, the adjuration of Jesus upon the tree was uttered one day and it was discovered withered the next morning.

It is supposed by some that Matthew's higher sense of the dignity of the Twelve led him to say in his account of the ambitious request of James and John[32] that "the mother of the sons of Zebedee" made the request, although Mark states categorically that James and John made their own request.[33]

In respect to discourse material, Matthew and Luke have much in common, yet significant changes take place in parallel sections. The Golden Rule is a case in point. The two versions are as follows:

Matt. 7. 12	*Luke 6. 31*
"All things, therefore, whatsoever you would that men should do to you, do thus also to them; for this is the law and the prophets."	"And just as you will that men should do to you, also do to them likewise."

The Golden Rule illustrates very well the freedom each writer had in phrasing his material. The addition, "for this is the law and the prophets," may be original or it may be an addition made by the evangelist to express his view that Jesus taught essentially the highest moral truth known among the Jewish people.[34] It is not desirable to

[30] 5. 1–20. [31] Mark 11. 12–14, 20–21; Matt. 21. 18–19.
[32] Matt. 20. 20–28. [33] Mark 10. 35–45.
[34] See also Matt. 10. 29 and Luke 12. 6, consulting Deissmann, *Light from the Ancient East*, p. 270–273; Matt. 11. 12 and Luke 16. 16; Matt. 12. 33 and Luke 6. 43–45, comparing the expanded form of the saying in Matt. 7. 16–20.

multiply illustrations, for those already adduced make clear to the student, first of all, that the evangelists exercised considerable freedom in their use of Jesus' sayings; secondly, that in repeated instances the modifications or expansions throw some light upon the view or the background of the writer, without seriously clouding any message that Jesus meant for his contemporaries; and, thirdly, that the Gospel record of Jesus' teaching, in its fourfold form, witnesses definitely to a developing thought about Jesus and his message.

The first Gospel preserves a view of Jesus which was characteristic of the Jewish Christian Church in Palestine or at least in Syria, perhaps about 75 A. D. The second Gospel represents not only an earlier period but a different group, namely, the church at Rome, composed of both Jewish and Gentile people, in the seventh decade of the first century. The third Gospel is designed for a circle of readers in the Greek world, probably for Macedonia in particular. Its date need not be set far from that of Matthew. The fourth Gospel, from a still later period, probably the last decade of the first century, is adapted to the thought of Greek Christians in Asia Minor.

The ethical message contained in them all is to be summed up in the concluding section of this study. That message was, of course, the message of the Man of Nazareth, addressed to people all of whom were within the Jewish Church, which was Jesus' own church. It was a message which dealt with very ancient moral truth, although some of this old truth needed and received new and striking emphasis. Because it was fundamentally true, essentially adapted to make human society more effective, and probably because the original message contained such a vital appeal to Jesus' contemporaries, these various settings devised by sympathetic followers of Jesus enhanced rather than dimmed the luster of the gem itself.

It is not too much to say that the moral message of Jesus is worth even more to readers who lived later than the first century A. D. because men of that century forged the old Aramaic Gospel anew, shaping it upon the anvils of their own experience, than it could be if brought down in a letter-perfect tradition without the tempering of those several generations of experience. The message of Jesus plus the experience of his followers constitutes the message of the Gospels.

The Ethical Teaching of Jesus

The moral thought of Jesus was not cast into any system. His was not the type of mind that delights in logical refinements, but, rather, he is seen to be a social prophet, busy in shepherding the neglected and in encouraging the poor and the disheartened. His voice was raised in prayer that the Lord of the harvest would send laborers with him into the field white but neglected. He called all the laboring and the burdened to his feet, where they should find rest. His thought was for the lost sheep of Israel's house, for the sick and not for the sound, for the sinful but not for the righteous.

The moral principles of Jesus have sometimes been systematized by later writers, but he himself appears in the Gospels to be the minister of all, whose eye was clear for the discernment of any need that was buttressed by faith, whose ear was attentive to the sigh of discouragement and to the faint cry for help. Jesus was, it may be, the poet of the waving wheat, of the rippling wave, of the lily of the field, of the falling sparrow, whose tragedy was not lost upon his Father, and of the glistening raindrop or the shining sun, which betokened to him the generous provision of God for his enemies as well as for his friends. But the mind of Jesus was not that of the systematic teacher.

The ethical teaching of Jesus comprises but few principles when all are brought together. Possibly those are right who think that in the phrase "Kingdom of God" may be found the one subject of his instruction. Many similes open the meaning of the Reign of God to readers of the Gospels, for its human aspects are many. Into this term Jesus put tremendous meaning, not exhausted by all four evangelists. The new order itself Jesus set up in his own time, selecting the men who were to form its nucleus and calling to others: "The Reign of God is here! Turn your feet toward it and cooperate with those who are seriously bringing in the new day!"

The Reign of God, in Jesus' thought, touches human life in all its phases. To the extent to which the sway of God prevails in human living, to that extent life will become wholesome, happy, effective and fruitful of good. Human life itself is, then, the field of ethics. Jesus' term, "the Reign of God," was taken from the lips of others, some of whom lived before the Master's time, but in Jesus' meaning it stood for a fellowship or community of men and women who were characterized by an absence of selfish insistence upon rights for their own sake, and by a devotion to all such constructive service of others as should bring out the best in human personality. Such a regime is least of all individualistic. The greatest in the community is the servant of all.

In the development of right relations with others, Jesus taught, the citizens of the Kingdom as sons of the Father would forgive readily, would practice nonresistance, would be generous and kind, not holding any grudge nor seeking revenge for evils done to them. None of these things were to be practiced by the son of the Father for its own sake, but for the sake of the community at large.

Explicit teaching of Jesus no doubt lay at the root of whatever universalism[35] is found in the Gospels. But one may doubt that Jesus included in his direct instruction of the Twelve all of the teaching which the more catholic of the evangelists based upon the actual expansion of "the Way" in their time. Clearly, in Jesus' thought, all men may become "sons of the Father," since all the race is one. Luke, in the sequel to his Gospel,[36] reports a word of Paul as to this unity of the race, which reflects the conviction of at least part of Jesus' followers in the sixth decade of his century. If it be asked whether Jesus' thought included the

---

[35] The term "universalism" as used here means the universal appeal of Christianity to the world, without distinction between Jew and Gentile. The term is in contradistinction to the term "nationalism," for example, as used in exposition of a certain attitude of the First Evangelist. See above, page 83. In the Acts of the Apostles Luke points out the prevalence of the narrower view in the Jerusalem church and traces the development of a real universalism in the ministry of Saint Paul.

[36] Acts 17. 26.

world-wide spread of his gospel the answer must be that in the highest probability it did. His brief ministry, however, did not offer him the opportunity to teach all that he had in mind.[37] It was to be expected that his followers would carry out his cardinal teaching to its logical conclusion, as light dawned upon them.

As all the evangelists testify, Jesus was at his best when teaching and illustrating the real values of life. Men, in his view, were immortal, worth "much more than many sparrows,"[38] worth, in fact, more than all the world itself.[39] Hence the Master rightly urged a consideration of values. "What can a man give for his soul?" Material and personal values are in reality incommensurable. The aim of the genuine disciple would be to develop the infinite character values which might lie forever undeveloped if the chief interest should be in crops and barns or in any sort of wealth that is subject to corrupting influences. Yet Jesus taught that his disciples should live in the world and take part in its activities. They should be real citizens of this world and enter rightly into its business and pleasures. Jesus' own contemporaries were surprised to find him "eating and drinking" and that too with all classes of people.

It was this fine balance between asceticism and license, between other-worldliness and commonness that aroused the interest of the many who heard Jesus gladly. He did not teach them in the way of

---

[37] This the Fourth Evangelist seems to think of as he records Jesus' saying (16. 12), "Still many things have I to say to you, but up to the present you are not able to stand them."

[38] Matt. 10. 31; Luke 12. 7.

[39] Matt. 16. 26; Mark 8. 36; Luke 12. 20.

their scribes. He was himself. A later follower of his urged his readers to "use the world as not abusing it," and in this advice Paul caught the spirit of his Master's life.

All the evangelists make much of the sublime appeal to personal religion which Jesus made the basis of all right-living. The prayer life of the Teacher is the dynamic center of his moral steadfastness. For with the early church the moral personality of Jesus was the great force behind his moral instruction. In the second generation of believers a well-instructed writer testified to the sublime fact that Jesus was tempted in every way, yet he did not at any point yield to temptation.[40] The person Jesus thus becomes at once the supreme sanction and the most effective example of the highest and noblest moral teaching ever brought to men. The modern student of Jesus' ethics need scarcely ask in what the originality of Jesus consisted. For the answer is found in the surpassing personality of the Teacher himself. He could and did repeat many moral truths of the past, but he glorified everything he used from that wonderful store-house. There is an intrinsic historical value in the words of those who returned from hearing the Master and exclaimed, "No one ever spoke like this man!"[41] Jesus spoke appreciatively of the insight of the prophets, but when he addressed his disciples in the prophets' very words it seemed to them it was with a new authority. In a real sense Jesus could not destroy the law or the prophets, for they were the Scriptures of his people and their

---

[40] Heb. 4. 15. [41] John 7. 46.

light was the brightest light on the moral pathway possessed by his contemporaries. But the person of Jesus in its charm of simplicity, in its force of persuasiveness, in its gentle but effective leadership, in its wonderful symmetry and depth of understanding—this is the very heart of the ethical teaching of Jesus.

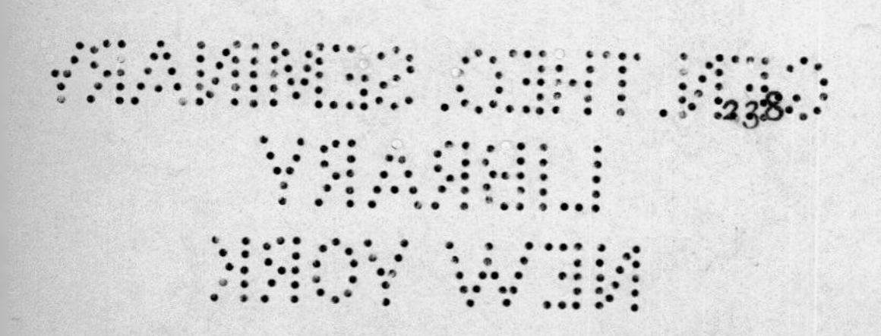